D N F

Did Not Finish

Andrew Todd
Iain Todd

twinbikerun

TwinBikeRun

Dedicated to Mum, Dad, Lesley, Nicola, Rebecca,
Bonnie, Charlie, Doc and Barney Xxx

CONTENTS

PREFACE

What does 'DNF' mean?

DNF refers to a competitor who started a race but 'did not finish' the race.

A DNF could be due to an injury, a twisted ankle or an accident that forces a competitor to stop. Or it could be due to a missed cut off time: some races require competitors to reach specific points within a set time. Or it could be due to an unforeseen problem.

Whatever the reason, however it happened, they did not finish. They DNF.

We are twin brothers. We have started many races we did not finish.

We are proud of every DNF we have received.

There is no failure in getting a DNF. Consider the words of John Wooden, former head basketball coach at the University of California, who wrote in his book *A Lifetime of Observations and Reflections On and Off the Court*:

"I had mistakes, plenty, but I had no failures. We may not have won a championship every year. We may have lost games. But we had no failures. You never fail if you know in your heart that you did the best of which you are capable."

This book is a celebration of the joy of doing the best you are capable of.

INTRODUCTION

Iain

It's 2011, and I am standing at the bottom of Africa's highest mountain, Kilimanjaro. Standing in front of me is an official whose job is to sign a certificate that would prove I had reached the summit. He asks me.

"Did you get to the top?"

I had not made it to the top. I attempted to reach the top, but I only made it as far as a large boulder 400 metres below the summit. At that point I told the other members of my group that I needed to go to the loo. As no loo was available, I would have to go behind a large boulder. In truth though, I didn't need the loo. I hid behind the boulder so that the others would not see me cry. I was feeling miserable. All I wanted to do was quit and go home.

"Did you get to the top?"

I don't answer; I don't want to answer. I want to be anywhere else but here. The official asks again.

"Did you get to the top?"

The mountain guide who led the trip replied for me.

"Iain did not get to the top."

The official says nothing; he opens a drawer and takes out a certificate and a stamp. He looks at me, and there is no emotion on his face. He stamps the certificate. I look at it. The certificate has a picture of Kilimanjaro on it, and on top of the page, he had stamped three large letters - "DNF."

"What does DNF mean?" I ask

"Is it not obvious?" He replies, "it means 'did not finish".

I feel depressed. How could I go home after not finishing? Before I left, I told friends, family and workmates I was off to Africa to conquer a mountain. How would I live down the shame of failure?

But then the official hands me the certificate, smiles and shakes my hand. "Don't worry. Congratulations. You reached your top!"

He was right. I'd finished, not at some arbitrary top, but my top. There was no need to be ashamed. None of my friends, family or workmates had climbed as far as I had. They hadn't even tried. I might not have finished, but at least I'd started.

I have tried to do many things, and I have not always reached the top. I attended a taster session to ride a track bike in a velodrome. During my ride, someone crashed into a wall above me. His bike slid down the track into mine. I fell off my bike and hit the ground hard. I bashed my shoulder and lost skin on my arm. In this case, my top was a very sore place at the bottom of steep banking.

Trying rugby, my coach told me that with the correct technique, I could tackle anyone. That was a lie: I tackled a man twice my size. My technique was perfect. I bounced off him and bashed my head off the hard ground of the rugby pitch. In this case, my top was a very sore head and a diagnosis of concussion.

Trying rock climbing, I went to a climbing centre and had to learn to attach a rope to my harness in two places. I tied the rope in only one place. I fell off the wall. Luck

ily the one place holding the rope was strong enough to break my fall. Unfortunately, that one place was my crotch. The instructor said it took balls to survive a fall like that. It certainly did. I wish I could say I learnt from this, but I did the same thing a few weeks later.

I hope this book will inspire you to reach your top.

Andrew

Do you want to hear the truth, or do you want a good story? That was a phrase my dad would say when I asked him a question.

Here's an example: when I was ten years old, I asked my dad, how do streetlights work? He replied, "Do you want to hear the truth, or do you want a good story?"

I said that I would like to hear a good story. He then told me that gnomes lived in the streetlights, and they would switch on the lights as soon as it got dark.

A couple of days later, I asked him again – how do streetlights work? But this time, I asked for the truth. So, he told me that a switch in the council headquarters controlled all the lights. And, every evening, my uncle, an electrician, was tasked with switching on the lights and every morning, he would switch them off. But sometimes, he'd forget, and that's why streetlights would shine in the middle of the day.

And I thought this was true; it sounded true. My uncle was an electrician. A light switch does turn on the lights. So why wouldn't there be a switch in the council to turn on all the lights?

I grew up on a small island in the Outer Hebrides, so it seemed feasible that one man could switch all the lights on. I didn't question this until I moved to Glasgow to attend University.

The first time the streetlights came on, I phoned home. I asked again. "How do streetlights work? Because one man and one switch can't control all the lights in Scotland."

And my dad asked if I wanted a good story or did I want the truth?

"The truth," I said.

He sighed and replied. "Okay, I'll tell you the truth, your uncle doesn't switch on all the lights in Scotland."

"I knew it," I exclaimed.

My Dad then added. "They have another man who switches them on for the mainland, so they don't have to connect a cable to the island".

I tell you this story because (a) you probably don't know how streetlights work (unless you are an electrician); (b) not everything I'm about to tell you happened.

I think it happened. It's based on my truth but, after reading Iain's record of the same events, it seems we have different realities.

Neither of us is intentionally making anything up but growing up with a father who would spin a yarn better than a Harris Tweed crofter means that we are not the most reliable narrators.

As an example - take our first triathlon. I remember coming last. And so does Iain. Yet we both can't be last. Of course, I could check the race result to find out the truth, but wouldn't you rather have a good story?

PART 1

CHAPTER ONE: PRIMARY SCHOOL

Iain

Elvis Presley died on Tuesday, 16th August 1977.

My Mum can remember that day quite clearly. She was in the Queen Mothers Hospital in Glasgow. She had just given birth to twins (Andrew and I) when a nurse told her that the King was dead.

She could tell by our loud tuneless screaming that neither Andrew or I had inherited any of the King's musical talent.

My birth was relatively easy, but Andrew's was more traumatic. When he popped out, he had the umbilical cord wrapped around his throat. The doctors had to act fast to save his life. Andrew blames me for it happening. He claims it was attempted murder. This could be true as I defy anyone to spend nine months enclosed in a small space with him and not want to strangle him.

Our parents were in their thirties when we were born. They had married three years previously. Our Mum, Catriona, was born on the Isle of Lewis in the Outer Hebrides. She lived there for most of her life until she moved to Glasgow in her twenties.

Our Mum is bilingual and speaks Gaelic fluently. Gaelic is the primary language of the island. She didn't learn English until she went to primary school. Then, to encourage her to learn English, the teachers would cane her if she spoke Gaelic. How times have changed, now millions of pounds are spent trying to encourage people to learn Gaelic.

Our Dad, Alan, was born and raised in Glasgow. He loved the outdoors and spent his youth trekking all over Scotland. In later life, to keep fit, he would walk three miles to and from his work every day. He would walk no matter what the weather - rain, hail or shine, which was annoying for Andrew and I. He'd make us walk when we wanted a lift to school in his car. I spent many school lessons cold and wet from walking in bad weather.

Andrew

To be fair to Dad, we didn't need a lift. We grew up in a house beside Stornoway Primary School. You could practically reach out and touch the school bell. It was faster to walk home than it was to reach the far end of the playground. We were the only kids who played red rover in the playground by crossing over our kitchen on the way to the other side.

But all that changed when we went to the Nicolson Institute, the secondary school, which was a whole five minutes away.

"We need to move," we'd plead.

"Why?" asked my Dad.

"Because we can't hear the school bell! If we can't hear it, how will we know to get to class?"

Which we thought was a good logical argument for moving, but he just bought both of us watches instead.

The other disadvantage of the Nicolson Institute was that it was on the same route our Dad used to get to work. That meant no matter what the weather – which in Stornoway was always a mix of rain, hail, rainy hail, haily rain or, in summer, one day of sunshine – we could never argue that we needed a lift as:

"It's not bad; I'm walking," said our Dad, as he pulled on full oilskins and a wetsuit, "so we don't need to drive."

3

Iain

I'm named Iain - like my cousin Iain, my cousin Iain and my other cousin Iain. I also have a cousin called John which is Gaelic for Iain. The Outer Hebrides doesn't have much variety when it comes to names. It's like surnames. Everyone is either a Macleod, a Macdonald, or a Maciver. My Mum was a Maciver. Which I have as a middle name.

Andrew is named after my Granddad on my Dad's side of the family. He, unfortunately, died from a heart attack at a young age; he was only 42. Supposedly, during his school days, he was an excellent runner who won many amateur athletic competitions. I wish I had inherited his love of running, but after studying a photo of him, all I've noticed is that I inherited his big nose.

My Granddad on my Mum's side also died at a young age from a heart attack. He was a fisherman. I wish I could have inherited his love of water, but after studying a photo of him, all I notice is that I inherited his big ears.

My Granny on my Mum's side recently turned 100. She received a card from the Queen, but she was more excited by a card from the internet card shop Moonpig. She said she preferred the picture on the front of that one.

My Granny on my Dad's side of the family died a few years ago. She had some strange opinions. One was a deep hatred of the horoscope writer, Russel Hardy. She never explained what it was about him that she hated so much, but when she got her daily newspaper, she would go straight to the horoscope and cut out his face and then throw it away. She must have had a bad horoscope experience when she was younger. Maybe he'd written she would come upon a great fortune, and it had never happened. If it did, she didn't give any of it to us.

Andrew

Despite my Granddad's running achievement, I never saw Dad

run. We know he must have because he played rugby when he lived in Glasgow, but he stopped running as soon as he arrived in Stornoway, which is ironic because my earliest memory involves running.

I say running, but actually, I was waddling. I had arrived from Glasgow at Stornoway Airport. I was aged three, and my Mum had flown up from Glasgow to start our new family life in the Outer Hebrides. Dad was at the airport to meet us. I was so excited to see him that I tried to run towards him.

Iain

My only memory of my time in Glasgow was falling down the stairs of our home. I'm sure Andrew pushed me. He denies it, but I suspect he was trying to get revenge for the umbilical cord incident.

Andrew

My only memory of Glasgow is pushing our cat at the top of the stairs and watching it fall down the stairs. I recently asked my Mum what the name of the cat was. She replied, "we didn't have a cat in Glasgow...."

Iain

I'd like to say we were lovely babies, but according to my Mum, we were "Hell!" Which is harsh. She could have sugared it a bit.

"You both never stopped screaming or crying. If one of you stopped crying, the other would start crying. If one of you stopped screaming, the other would start screaming. I never got a moments peace."

We left Glasgow when my Dad was offered a job in the Outer Hebrides. He was keen to take it, but my Mum didn't want to go back to the island. She eventually succumbed and said, "okay, but only for a year" That year has now become 40 years. Although Mum is still determined to one day move back to the mainland.

We arrived in Lewis in 1980. Our first house on the island was a croft house in a small community called Point, the worst town to live in because all conversations go like this.

"Where are you from?"

"Point"

[Stretches hand to the horizon.]

"Are you from over there?"

My Dad had a job in the Harris Tweed industry, and my Mum did part-time work in newsagents and the local hospital. Unfortunately, I don't remember much about my early years there other than fleeting glimpses of the past.

I remember getting our first pets - a sheep each called Donald and Shona.

Andrew

Iain's wrong. They were called Dougie and Georgie.

Iain

A sheep is not a particularly good pet. It does not respond to commands. Donald would not fetch, sit or wait. He could only do two things he would eat grass, and if he was hungry, he would say "baa". Shona was no better. She never once responded to her name when called. She showed complete indifference to us as owners.

One day we came home, and the sheep were gone. Mum said they had gone to a better place where they'd be happier. In later life, she admitted the better place was my uncles' belly. He chopped them up and ate them.

After sheep, we stuck with cats as pets. We didn't eat them

Andrew

After intense questioning, I remember our Dad said that the 'better place' was Barbados, and when we asked how they'd crossed the Atlantic, he said they'd gone by yacht. He then took us down to the harbour and pointed out the yachts they'd used because they naturally had one each. For a couple of years afterwards, I would look out for Dougie and Georgie's yachts, and every time I'd think: "If they've gone to Barbados, why are the yacht's back in Stornoway?" Finally, my Dad said they were back on holiday, which, when your six, made perfect sense.

Iain

Some of my memories of being young are:

I remember power cuts were common. We'd lose all lighting and power in the house. My Dad would light a fire for heat and light. Whilst we waited for the electricity to return, Mum would tell stories to try and entertain us.

I remember when my cousin visited us. We went to a local playpark. My cousin went on the swings. I pushed her, but I didn't realise that what swings one way can swing back the other way. So she swung forward and then swung back into my face. I broke my nose and had to be rushed to hospital to get it fixed. My cousin is now a doctor. I like to think I had a hand or nose in her choice.

I remember Mum shouting at us because we tended to wander off looking for adventure but forgot to come back in time for dinner.

But most of all, I remember feeling happy and loved.

Andrew

My Mum had a simple approach to buying clothes for us. First, buy everything twice, so there were no arguments about who wore what she would buy everything in two different colours.

If you look at old photos, you will see I'm in the blue parka. Iain's in the purple parka. I'm wearing a red jumper; Iain is in a black jumper. It was a clever system; it made it easier to tell which of us was which.

But there was one downside. If he looked stupid in his clothes, then that meant I must look stupid too. I can hardly laugh at what he's wearing when I'm wearing the same thing.

We still wear similar clothes. The problem with being brought up wearing the same things is that we now share a similar taste in fashion. I check what he's wearing before meeting him if we both turn up wearing the same clothes.

The upside more than matches the downsides of looking alike. Take glasses. We've both needed glasses since primary school when he tripped me up in the playground, and I banged my head on the ground and got dirt in my eye. A trip to the optician led to discovering that one eye was wonky, and I would need glasses for the rest of my life. The same trip also led Iain to need glasses because the next time he ran through the playground, I tripped him up in revenge and, no sooner can you say, "I should have eaten more carrots", he was at the optician finding out he had a wonky eye too.

Iain

I have no recollection of tripping Andrew. We both have astigmatism, a common vision problem caused by an error in the shape of the cornea. It is not caused by tripping someone up.

Andrew

The best way to buy glasses is to bring Iain to the opticians too. If I need to decide between Elton John flamboyance or monocle simplicity, I ask Iain to try them. I can then see what I would look like with them.

When we did wear the same clothes, it was difficult to tell us apart. At primary school, we both played football for the school team. I played in defence. He played in midfield. He scored goals. I let them in (I wasn't very good). But whenever the local paper printed our match results, it would always say I scored when it was Iain. Worse, for Iain, the one time I did score, they printed my name correctly. I was named as one of the top strikers in the league while only ever scoring one goal.

Most people at school did not try to tell us apart, which was reflected in our names. We were usually called the same variant of the "Todd Twin" or "one of the twins" or "Big Nose" (Iain, clearly.). This was okay until we discovered girls. Or, more accurately, one girl discovered Iain.

It was Valentine's Day, and there was a girl who lived in the next street. I fancied her, but I'd never spoken to her but, when I looked out our living room window, I could see she was walking into the garden, carrying an envelope. "She's dropping off a card," I thought, "for me". Clearly, she'd been impressed by the sight of my blue parka.

She posted the envelope. I ran to the door. She'd already gone, but I ripped the envelope open.

"Roses are red; violets are blue; I would like to K.I.S.S. you."

Not the best rhyme, but I could forgive her as I could see the glazed glass of the front door that she was coming back. She'd seen me, and now she wanted to turn her rhyme into reality.

She knocked on the door.

I opened it.

She looked at me.

I looked at her, and she said:

"Are you Iain or Andrew?"

And I said "Andrew", and she got out a pen and asked for her card and wrote Iain's name on it.

"Can you make sure he gets it?" She asked.

I said yes, closed the door and then binned it.

Though looking back, I do admire her. Most people would have said nothing, and it would only be on her deathbed, years later, would she turn to me, her husband, and laughingly admit what had happened. But no, she needed to make 100% sure that I knew that this card was not for me.

Iain

At primary school, there were two types of physical exercise. The first was the official physical education lessons. The second was the games and sports played before, during and after school.

I would have P.E. lessons twice a week. Each session lasted one hour. At the start of the class, our female teacher would make all the boys stand against a wall. She'd then let the girls play games for 40 minutes whilst the boys watched. She'd then stop them from playing so the boys could play for 20 minutes in the end.

She once made the boys stand for the whole hour without getting any exercise at all. I hated her and her class.

Years later, I decided to get my revenge on her for all the missed classes. I had a job as a paperboy. She was one of my customers. She liked The Scotsman newspaper, but she hated the Daily Record. Whenever there were no copies of the Scotsman in stock, I'd put a Daily Record through her door instead. It was a petty thing to do, but I felt good doing it.

I realise now that what I did was wrong. She was doing a good thing by giving the girls more exercise than the boys. Boys played football before school, every break time, and after school. Girls, on the other hand, had no opportunity for sport except at lessons. There were no facilities for them to play at breaks and no encouragement from any other teacher to exercise. I was not discriminated against by losing P.E. time. I was privileged to get every other bit of time. I'm now sorry I gave her the Daily Record. It's a crap newspaper.

Andrew

My first sporting memory is watching a team in green and

white winning the Scottish Cup against a team in orange. I loved football and wanted to follow the team that won. They were Celtic, and that was about the only thing they won in the next fifteen years as their rivals, Rangers, dominated Scottish football until 2000. I didn't know it at the time but choosing Celtic in the Western Isles was like ordering a steak in a vegan restaurant. Everyone on the island supported Rangers because the Isle of Lewis is to Protestants what the Vatican is to Catholics.

Lewis is a very religious island. Sunday or the Sabbath is a holy day, and no shops would open, the swings in playparks would be tied up, and even clotheslines would be cut if anyone dared to hang their underwear out on the Lord's day.

It was tediously DULL.

Imagine a day when nothing happened. Slowly. But it was just a standard 24 hour day. The Stornoway sabbath started when the minister went to bed on a Saturday night, and it didn't end until he got up on a Monday morning.

On the Sabbath, I was supposed to go to church and do nothing else. Even watching T.V. was banned, though not in my house. There was a football highlight show on ITV on a Sunday afternoon. My Dad would watch it.

In recent years, the airport and ferry companies have run services to allow people to leave the island on a Sunday. Iain and I inadvertently ended up on the first Sunday sailing. We were in Stornoway, saw a Sunday sailing and booked it, not knowing it was the first. At the ferry terminal, 20 people in black suits and heavy tweed coats were silently protesting – because, naturally, shouting was banned on Sunday. Besides them, a hundred people were clapping to show their support for the new service. Onboard we hid below deck; while we supported the new service, we didn't want to be in the photo they'd use in the local paper under the headline "Heathens Leave Island. Destination: Hell!".

I love the Stornoway Sabbath. It provides a day each week when I know I don't need to do anything. However, the Stornoway version is too extreme. I will break the rules a little.

In many ways, growing up in Stornoway was a glimpse not just into the recent past but into an older past too. While the mainland moved with the times and Sunday became the weekend rather than a special day itself, Stornoway remembered that the Sabbath meant something. It was a reminder that you should spend one day a week doing something different, whether resting, praying or tying up children's swings (lest Satan tempts them to swing on the Sabbath).

There's a lesson here for triathletes – have a rest day. It's just as important to stop as it is to start training. Pushing to do something every day is not always progress.

Maybe, that's the lesson our first P.E. teacher was trying to teach the boys when she made them do nothing for most of the lesson? Maybe she was teaching me patience?

Or she was an old boot.

It's one or the other.

Iain

She isn't the only teacher I need to apologise to. I also need to apologise to my favourite primary school teacher, Mr Gordon Matheson. He was the one who introduced me to football: my first sporting love.

I promised him that one day I'd play for the Scottish national football team. I failed. I'm not sure where it went wrong. My primary school team won the inter-school football competition every year. This was in no small part due to having a striker in our team who was twice the size of the opposition players.

I didn't feature in the secondary school team because they had a strict rule about only playing people with talent and ability.

This rule has hindered my football career. If it wasn't for talent discrimination, I could have won 100 caps.

At University, I had one season in the University's first division. Not because I was talented but because of an administration error. I think the admins thought my team's application to play in division 7 looked like a 1. My team lost every single week, and I didn't score a single goal. Which I think qualifies me to know what it would be like to play for Scotland.

After University. I played in a Glasgow five a side league. I quit after spotting a sign on the noticeboard that said, "the following teams have been given warnings for violent conduct." Which went on to list every single team I was due to play against.

I did once come close to getting a call up to the national team. One day, I was walking along a road, and the Scotland manager of the time, Walter Smith, was walking towards me. We would have collided if I hadn't jinked out the way at the last moment. As I moved past him with ease, I noticed him look at me, and I like to think that he thought, "what poise, what balance, what a player". But as he didn't know who I was, he couldn't call me up to the squad.

I have one last teacher I need to apologise to — a science teacher in Secondary School. I want to apologise for killing his goldfish. He thought Goldie the goldfish died of natural causes. Instead, Goldie died when I fed him anti-acne tablets. I hope, when he flushed Goldie down the loo, he noticed how acne-free his skin was.

Andrew

My only other sporting memory from primary school was sitting in the Western Isles Hospital talking to a friend who had broken his arm riding his BMX. He lived on the highest street in town. He started cycling at the top, but as he gathered speed heading downhill, he realised the brakes didn't work. He tried to grab a streetlight to stop. He crashed.

His cast was covered in signatures. Everyone was going out to see him. Other boys in school were trying to replicate his streetlight shenanigans, I'm not sure what they thought would happen differently, and a spate of broken arms followed. And all I could think was: "How cool would it be to have a BMX?". And that's how I got my first bike. I didn't tell my Mum and Dad what had happened to him. If they'd known, I'd never have got a BMX.

CHAPTER TWO:
SECONDARY SCHOOL

Iain

I realised at secondary school I was good at starting things but not finishing them.

I've mentioned the rugby coach who told me, "With the correct technique, you can tackle anyone", but I didn't mention that afterwards; Andrew told me that people with concussions die eight hours after they get concussed. I stayed up late that night, watching the clock tick down to my impending death. Jools Holland was on TV. My death was going to occur halfway through the show, which annoyed me. A band I liked was due to play at the end of the show. I never played rugby again.

My sporting failures did not end with rugby. I also failed at running. When I was at school, there was a road that ran along the front of it. But since then, the school has been demolished, and so has the road. This is sad for me, as it was a road that had a special place in my sporting heart. It was where I became the fastest boy in school history.

When I saw the road was gone, I felt how Andy Murray would feel if Wimbledon was knocked down and replaced by a Tesco Metro. He'd probably need a sit-down – although that might be due to his dodgy hip.

My achievement happened during my fifth year of secondary school. During PE lessons, the class would take part in a 100m race. The course was set up on the road outside the school.

The PE teacher picked one of the other boys to go out with a measuring wheel to mark the start and the end of the course. Once it was set up, the class lined up at the beginning of the course.

I didn't warm up before the race. This was the 1990's. Warming up hadn't been invented yet.

We didn't have blocks, so it was a standing start. The gym teacher blew his whistle. I started running. I swiftly covered the first 50m and was soon near the front, running alongside a boy wearing Joe Bloggs jeans. He'd forgotten his shorts, but he didn't care as he knew the jeans made him the coolest guy in our year. I knew he'd slow down towards the end as he wouldn't want to get the jeans sweaty.

In the last 10m, I was Eric Carmen. No, not the kid from South Park – that's Eric Cartmen. Eric Carmen wrote and sang All By Myself. [*NOTE: I thought that reference would be less obscure, but as I've gone to the trouble of googling "who sang All By Myself?" then I'm keeping the reference in.*]

And then I was over the line. The teacher checked his watch and said, "wow, your time is unbelievable. You might have the school record." I couldn't believe it. The teacher couldn't believe it. My fellow pupils couldn't believe it.

The teacher nor I knew at the time that the boy who'd been sent out to mark the course didn't know how to use a meter roller, so instead of measuring the course accurately, he'd guessed how far 100m was. So he'd created a course of 87m.

This was discovered when another PE teacher heard about the time and realised that a slow runner could not possibly have run the time claimed.

I was the fastest boy in the school's history for about ten minutes, and then it was annulled.

I was so embarrassed I vowed not to run again.

Andrew

Except that's not what happened. It was me who did it. I was 14 when I, and not Iain, broke the 100m sprint world record by sprinting home in 9.5 seconds. I could have run faster. Conditions were tricky. We didn't have a running track at our school, so all sprints had to take place on the road in front of the school gates. A teacher would stand at the end of the road and stop the traffic from giving us a minute to run clear before angry drivers would start to beep their horns.

Also, I was wearing Adidas Sambas trainers, which were perfect for playing five a side football but had, as far as I know, never been Carl Lewis's first choice to contest the Olympics. They wouldn't have been his second or third choice either, given he was a professional athlete with access to global brands, and I needed a pair of trainers that would last from birthday to Christmas because I only had one pair of shoes. Sambas were versatile. (And smelly).

I must admit it was also windy. And wet. So not ideal conditions for a world record. But this was Stornoway in the Western Isles, and every day is windy and wet. However, that only makes us run faster because everyone knows the cure to pneumonia is to outrun it.

Unfortunately, even with these impediments, I didn't break our school record while I broke the Olympic record. That stood at 9.1 seconds because I wasn't the first to finish that day. That time belonged to the boy who came first. I wasn't even in the top three. I was sixth. And I have to admit that, yes, Iain was ahead of me. But, technically, he was faster, better than me and now a world record holder. I can only guess that this is how Venus Williams must feel when she looks at her trophy cabinet, one of the most decorated in tennis, and then pops round to see her sister, Serena.

I was happy, though. It's not every day you beat the world record. Unless you're Adam Peaty swimming the 200m breaststroke, and every time you break the world record is every time you go for a swim. Just imagine how fast he could be if he learned how to swim the crawl?!?

Unfortunately, my record didn't last long. A formal enquiry was launched, which is an elaborate way of saying the PE teacher, scratched his head and said, "This ain't right".

You would have thought he would be pleased that he had found a golden generation of natural sprinters. But he called over the two fastest runners and asked them to run again.

They lined up. Standing start, none of the blocks nonsense that the professional use. How can you run faster if you have to get up first? If you're already standing, then you're going to have an advantage over someone kneeling.

He blew his whistle, and they smashed it. 8.9 seconds. We were witnessing history. Some people say it'll be another hundred years and at least four generations of evolution for humankind to ever run so fast – we did it twice in five minutes.

"Well, it's not my stopwatch," said the teacher.

"Maybe, we're just really fast," I suggested.

He took one look at my Adidas Sambas and trackie bottoms – as I'd forgotten to bring shorts. Also, I still had my glasses on because otherwise, I'd never have managed to run in a straight line. And he knew that I knew that I had never shown any athletic ability whatsoever and could only say:

"Right, either we've got a generation of Ben Johnson's, or one of your wee b******ds didn't measure the course out correctly. So who's got the metre stick?"

And with that, he grabbed the metre stick and meticulously laid it end to end 100 times along the road.

He came back.

"It's only 87 meters – you can all run again".

And that's how I lost the world record after just five minutes. Although, of course, it turned out I never had it in the first place. But, for five minutes, I was ever so briefly the fastest man on the planet, except for the five ahead of me, but they cheated, so they don't count.

Iain

The teachers at our school were a mixed bunch.

My physics teacher was a drunk. He had no idea who anyone in his class was. At the start of each year, he would take a photo of the class. At the school parents evening, he pointed at the class photo and asked my parents: "Which one's yours?"

My history teacher used to tell fat kids at the front of the class to move to the back as they were blocking the view of the other pupils.

My technical teacher gave me a bit of wood to make a model boat. He then used my bit of wood to demonstrate how to do it. When I gave it to him for assessment, he said it was rubbish and gave me a "D." It was his work.

My swimming teacher couldn't swim, but that didn't stop him from teaching it. He had three rules for swim class.

No dive bombing!

No kit, no swim!

No verrucas!

A verruca is a wart on a foot. It's commonly caught off someone else who has one. It was widespread in the 1980s so, to prevent the spread of verrucas, swimming pools had a small foot sized sink in the ground at the exit of changing rooms. The sink would contain a red chlorine-like liquid.

Despite using the foot sink, I got a verruca. Andrew got a verruca. Most of my school got a verruca later. I learnt that one of the biggest causes of verrucas was the foot sink because leisure centres didn't clean them well or often enough.

It put me off from going swimming. I didn't like the wart. I didn't like the wee red pool of disease. I didn't like the heavy smell of chlorine in the air. I didn't like all the people in the pool swimming past or across me. I hated everything about swimming.

I vowed never to swim ever again.

Andrew

I hated swimming. I hated all sports – except one, football.

Most of all, I hated running and one type of running in particular: cross country.

Strawberry Hill might sound like a Clint Eastwood film. A war movie about impossible odds and unimaginable suffering set in Vietnam starring Bradley Cooper clenched jawed and doing his serious voice. It's not, but it certainly felt like it.

Every week, around April and May, a minibus would leave our school, the Nicolson Institute, and drive five minutes to the Lews Castle Grounds, which is the only area of woodland on the Isle of Lewis. The island is so windswept; there's little point in planting trees. It would only take a winter storm for most of them to be uprooted and blown to the mainland. The Castle Grounds is the one area where, in a sign of what billionaires did before private jets were invented, a man, James Matheson, bought the island and decided that he would turn part of the town into a forest. Money doesn't grow on trees, but it can grow into trees.

This area of ground, the Castle Grounds, was named because it was the grounds of Matheson's castle, which overlooks the town, is filled with muddy paths and trails. One starts at the castle and then proceeds upwards until it climbs to the top of a hill called Strawberry Hill before looping back round to the start. I don't know why it's called Strawberry Hill. Strawberries have as much chance of growing on Lewis as a giraffe does of winning a limbo contest.

And I say 'hill', but it's not much of a hill. But, when you're 14, it felt like Everest.

We would be driven to the car park, thrown out the minibus and told to run up and round the hill no matter the weather – or athletic ability.

30 kids. Three of them liked running, 20 didn't, and seven only wanted to know a Strawberry if it was a flavour of ice cream.

We would run. Well, walk. Well, we gasped straight up the hill until we were out of sight of the PE teacher. We'd then stop. Wait for the first runner to come back, then wait a bit longer not to raise suspicions and then jog back down the hill in a re-spectable mid-pack place.

That was PE. A never-ending attempt by the teacher to avoid playing football. Because football was all I wanted to play. It was all we all wanted to play. But every year, the PE teachers would design a curriculum that had everything but football.

We would play hockey in the summer on a pitch with more holes than a championship golf course and slope so steep that if you missed the ball when someone passed it to you, it was likely to gather enough speed to get to Australia.

We played rugby. I say played; I tried to avoid permanent para-lysis as we would play with the senior team and be tackled by 17 stone men who believed you should find courage and walk off a broken neck.

We even tried track and field. But the sandpit was made of concrete as no sand would hold in the fierce Lewis winds, and even our PE teachers baulked at performing a triple jump into industrial tarmacadam.

Yet, week after week, they persisted in the face of utter in-difference. I couldn't understand at the time why they kept trying to make us play sports we didn't want to play. Why not just give us football? It's what we wanted? Every week we'd groan at the latest attempt to show us how to throw a discussion or how to shoot a hoop with a basketball. "Sir, can we not just play football?"

Not that playing football was without its dangers. One of the venues was the Acres Boys Club – a metal shed beside the school with a small five a side pitch and a central heating system that worked entirely on 50p coins. Anyone could hire it, but no one would heat it unless they were playing. Which was okay in summer, or a single week in June as it was known in Stornoway, but it meant Arctic expeditions used the club for cold weather practice for the rest of the year.

We would play in the morning and, before we started, the teacher would inspect each of the corners of the pitch and declare: "Don't run into the bottom left corner. At least, not until the heating kicks in."

Before, he would then ask: "Does anyone have a 50p coin as I only have two twenties and a ten?"

Ice would form in the corners. Nine times out of 10, we'd play less like Diego Maradona and more like Torvill and Dean performing the Bolero.

Playing outside was no better. There were no pitches in Stornoway that were level. Every pitch might as well have been built on the side of Strawberry Hill.

Yet we kept asking for football, and the PE teachers kept offering every other sport but football.

Iain

It was during secondary school that I got my first bike. It was for my first job – a paperboy. The bike was a racer. Which is now known as a road bike, but that was not a term I was aware of back then. All bikes were road bikes. Where else other than a road would you cycle?

Andrew got a bike too. Also, a racer.

Andrew

It wasn't a racer. It was a white BMX. I remember it because I used to work as a paperboy, and I would hang plastic bags filled with the papers from the flat handlebars. And I remember it distinctly because a bag snapped one day, and it got caught in the front wheel and threw me off to smash my face against the road. A passing car took pity on me and drove me to hospital, which was a problem because that's where my mum worked, and I had to admit what I'd done. If I thought my face hurt, it was nothing compared to what happened after my mum found out I'd been trying to balance two plastic bags containing 30 newspapers off the handlebars of my bike.

Iain

Now, I should mention that some people believe that twins share a special psychic connection.

The book "The Encyclopedia of Superstitions" says:

"It is a widespread belief that twins, especially identical twins, are united by a strong bond of sympathy that each knows when danger or misfortune threatens the other, even when they are separated."

A few years ago, I experimented to see whether this statement was true – would I feel anything if Andrew was in pain or danger?

We did it in a very scientific way – we formed a comedy double act. Like a cheuchter Ant and Dec but without their comedy timing, jokes or ability. We were so bad the only TV shows we could have hosted would've been Britain's Got No Talent or I'm Not a Celeb Leave Me Right Here.

I admit that this was not the best idea I've ever had. But I did have a genius idea for a joke. An idea that couldn't fail – we'd do an experiment on stage where I'd get an audience member to hit Andrew with a rolled-up newspaper whilst I looked away. I would then try to guess where he'd been struck. I thought it would be comedy slapstick gold. It wasn't.

We went to a poetry night that allowed a bit of comedy to test the idea out, because I reasonably thought nothing wrong could happen at a poetry night.

When it came to our turn, we stood up and proceeded to tell a few gentle gags to get the audience warmed up. The audience laughed and applauded, but as they'd just spent 90 minutes listening to poetry, I think they would have welcomed anything that wasn't more poetry.

I stepped forward and asked for a volunteer from the audience. No one volunteered, so I looked around the room and saw a man sitting by himself. He looked harmless enough. This was mistake number one – a man by himself at a poetry night must be a solid gold mental rocket of the highest order.

I invited him on stage and realised he was bigger than I thought. He was built like a rugby player. He was also a bit drunk. No worries – I'll just continue the show. I handed him the newspaper and asked him to roll it up. This was mistake number two – never give a man a weapon and ask him to load it himself. He rolled it very tight. So tight it was now more substantial than a wooden baton.

I looked at Andrew. I could see fear in his eyes. I looked at the audience member. I could see violence in his eyes. So I did what any loving brother would do. I turned to the man and said, "I'm going to look away. Hit my brother as hard as you like and wherever you like!"

This was mistake number three – I shouldn't have turned my back on the scene of the crime.

I shouted, "Hit him".

There was silence and then a big THWACKKKK sound before

more silence....like the silence you get after a nuclear bomb has detonated, but the blast hasn't reached you yet. Then the audience gasped: Andrew screamed. He'd been struck in the balls; he was now my twin sister rather than a brother.

If I were psychic, I would have felt something. I felt nothing. The audience member hit Andrew again. THWACKKKK....S-CREAM...THWACKKKKK, THWACKKK....SCREAM! Each time he was hit, I felt nothing.

As Andrew lay on the floor writhing in pain. His crown jewels have been pulverised. I asked myself, "Are twins psychic?"

The answer is definitely, and for me, thankfully: "No".

Andrew

You would have thought I would never agree to do this ever again, but we did it in Manchester a few weeks later. Someone in the crowd recorded the gig. It's on YouTube if you want to find it. I've never watched it. I'm worried about getting PTSD. Afterwards, we split up over creative differences. I wanted to perform in comedy clubs, and he thought we were getting a bigger audience in A&E departments.

Iain

During our paper rounds, we'd hang the bag of newspapers from the handlebars of our bikes. But, of course, the more papers we had to deliver, the harder it was to balance a bag on the handlebars.

Due to the Stornoway sabbath, there were no Sunday papers on a Sunday. However, the Sunday papers arrived on a Monday, which meant I had two days' worth of papers to carry.

There should be a special place in hell reserved for anyone who asks a paperboy to deliver the Sunday Times. Every week it caused me problems. It was so thick, and I could barely hang it from my bars.

I suspect Andrew's bag burst because he was carrying The Sunday Times. The Sunday Times might be "The Sunday Papers", but it's also an accident waiting to happen.

Thinking back, did I feel a psychic connection at that point? I did feel something. I felt a pang of hunger. It was late, and I hadn't eaten since lunchtime. Andrew went to the hospital, and I went home for my dinner.

I loved that bike. We were inseparable until we quite literally separated. It snapped in two, which was annoying as I was riding it at the time.

I vowed never to ride a bike again.

By the end of secondary school, I had started and finished my swim, bike and running careers.

Andrew

I can't even say I tried. I didn't swim unless it was a PE lesson. I didn't run unless it was to chase a football, and I couldn't ride a bike without having an accident. So I left school without any sporting ambitions at all.

CHAPTER THREE:
UNIVERSITY

Andrew

I spent my first three years of university doing anything but running, cycling or swimming.

I went to Glasgow. Iain went to Edinburgh. They were our cities, and the border lay somewhere on the M8 motorway near Bathgate. It was the first time I ever had a room of my own and the first time I didn't see Iain every hour of every day.

Finally, I could get a good night's sleep. At home, we shared a bunk bed. He had the top bunk, and I had the bottom. And I can confirm that just before anyone goes to sleep, their body spasms because every night, just as I was going to sleep, the bunk would shake, and the headboard would bang. Confirming Iain had fallen asleep. Unfortunately, this would wake me up from my attempt to nap, and I'd spent a long time trying to drop off again.

I studied law. It was interesting. I've written three books on legal matters. I suspect you don't love Scottish conveyancing as much as me. I'd better not dwell too long on it as you want to know about me failing at sports than failing to spot an incorrect application to the Lands Tribunal of Scotland under section 98 of the Title Conditions (Scotland) Act 2003.

Nothing much happened sports-wise until, in the fourth year, I decided I had exams to pass, and the only way I was going to do that was to get into a routine, and one part of that routine should be to do something other than sit in a library for eight hours a day. I was going to get fit, and the only way I knew how to get fit was to workout. And the only way to see if I was working out successfully was to weigh myself every week and see if I was putting on weight.

I was scientific. I picked a scale in the gym. I measure myself. 11 stone. I decided that one pound a week was a reasonable target and that, if I did that, by the time I finished studying, I'd be 12 stone.

I needed some exercise. So, I did what everyone does when they start. I bought an issue of Men's Health that promised to "Transform My Life With Just Three Moves", and I set out a simple plan. First, I would run for 20 minutes on a treadmill to warm up. I'd then go to the weight room and ignore Men's Health because even three moves sounded complicated. So, instead, I'd use each machine twice, going in a circuit until I'd finished 15 repetitions on each one.

I then bought a weights belt because I read they help prevent back injuries, which was true. I didn't once get a back injury while wearing it. Equally, I didn't once try any weight heavy enough to crack an egg, never mind my spine, but you can't be too careful, you know.

And I started to workout. I was going to transform myself.

Iain

I studied Computing at the University of Edinburgh. I remember my first day at university. I was informed I had to do a maths course as part of my degree.

I asked, "Why? I'm here to study Computing."

The tutor replied that it was a requirement of the British Computer Society.

I said, "Why? I'd rather learn something useful."

He looked at me and said, "Stop arguing. Just sign up for the maths course!"

At the end of the year, I did the maths exam. I answered every single question and included my working out. Unfortunately, I got a score of 0/30, and the tutor wrote, "This shows no knowledge of maths whatsoever."

Since then, I've had a successful IT career. And I've never needed maths.

You don't need to go to University to be successful. You need to work hard. People will judge you on what you achieve in life and not by what bit of paper you hold.

Andrew

My first run in my new routine was on a treadmill. It was boring. I tried running faster. Still boring, but now I was sweating. I tried increasing the incline to make it feel like I was running up a hill. Not only was this boring, too, I was also catching the attention of everyone else in the gym as it looked like I was holding on for dear life. And I was sweating — so much sweat. And I'd only been running for two minutes.

Next to me, another runner was sweat-free and running faster. How long had they been running for? One hour. Bloody hell. I had now been running for three minutes, and I was bored. I started to wonder why Gyms have mirrors?

There is nothing worse in a gym than catching someone's eye in the mirror. Why are they staring at you? Why are you staring at them? Why are we both still staring? Oh God, I should glance away and pretend I didn't notice them. Except, unlike in the street, when you accidentally catch the eye of a stranger, you can't move on a treadmill. You have to keep running beside them as they run beside you, and you both try not to acknowledge each other is there.

I've now been running for five minutes. I must have run a mile by now. Roger Bannister took four minutes, and that was decades ago. I check the distance: 1 km. A kilometre? What's a kilometre? How many miles is that? Two? Is a kilometre shorter than a mile? I'm now not just bored and sweaty – I'm also doing maths. This is awful. I'm going nowhere, I've still got fifteen minutes left to run, and my mind is trying to work out how much of a fraction 1000 metres is of sixteen hundred.

But I had committed to this new routine. For ten weeks, three times a week, I torture myself by making myself run on a treadmill. I hate it. I still do. There is nothing natural about running on the spot. In pre-historic times we learned to run by either running towards an enemy or running away from a dinosaur. No one ran on the spot, at least not long enough before a T-Rex ate them. The only people who run on the spot are mime artists, and no one should take inspiration from a mime unless you ever want to know how to react when you're shot.

And it was working. I'd said myself a target of gaining a pound a week, and every week I gained a pound until at the end of term, I was 12 stone and could lift more than I could ten weeks before, which was pointless because I don't lift things. I didn't need more muscles. It was not making any difference to my life to lift a larger set of metal plates than I could ten weeks previously. It was a pointless exercise. But the running, despite its mind-numbing boredom, had an effect. I was running more when playing football. I couldn't pass a ball, trap a ball or score a goal, but I could make up for it by running around more of the pitch than anyone other than the Duracell bunny.

And then one night, I thought. I could run home from football. There's no need to catch the underground. I'll just run. It's only a couple of miles, and I run longer than that on a treadmill. So, after an hour of football, I grabbed my backpack and slowly jogged through Glasgow from just north of the city centre to the west end. And it wasn't boring. It didn't involve running on the spot. It was liberating. I was running for a purpose. I was running home!

And that was the lightbulb moment: the Eureka in a bathtub moment. Running was a journey: a start and an end. If you're going to move, then you have to move. And then the lightbulb fell in the bathtub and electrocuted all my good intentions because, for the next 15 years, I treated every run like a treadmill.

Iain

Do you remember your first time?

Were you nervous? I bet you worked up a sweat, but you didn't last long.

Did lots of people see you do it?

I'm talking about your first run. What do you think I was talking about?

I used to run at the gym. I would do ten minutes on the rowing machine, ten minutes on a bike and then a ten-minute run.

Which, to me, seemed like a lot of exercises. Nowadays, it sounds like a warm-up session.

During this time, I went on a date, and my date asked me what I liked to do for fun. I replied that I had gone to the gym.

She laughed at me and said, "You go to the gym?" in a tone that was very, very doubtful.

I felt embarrassed. Why did she think I didn't go to the gym? I did 10 minutes on each machine! I bet that was 10 minutes more than most people.

I vowed I would try to do more than 10 minutes, but there was one problem. I got very bored in the gym. I struggled to do the ten minutes on the machines, let alone try for more.

I decided to run outside instead. I lived next to a park. I vowed to run around the park. So on a sunny spring day, I changed into my running gear and then procrastinated about leaving my flat.

What if anyone I know sees me? They will point and laugh. I bet even people who don't know me will say, "look at that man trying to run. Doesn't he look funny"

I put my clothes back on and didn't run that day.

The next day I tried again, but this time I decided to run at night. That way, no one would see me.

After 30 minutes of my brain trying to convince me not to go running, I made it to the front door.

I stepped outside. I didn't know what to do. Should I start running immediately? Should I go fast, should I go slow. Where will I run to?

I ran around the park. I tried to avoid people, which is pretty straightforward. I'm 6ft 1 inch tall. It was dark. Most people who see a 6ft 1-inch man running towards them in a park at night run away.

Andrew

My first outdoor run started well but went downhill fast. Literally, Glasgow University is on a hill, and every direction to run in is downhill.

I ran down Gibson Street, a particularly steep street that could be used for skydiving practice. I ran in a straight line until I hit the M8 motorway, and then I turned left until I got to Great Western Road, a long road leading through Glasgow Westend out to the country, and I ran along with it until I could turn left at Byres Road and return to the university. It was an almost perfect square.

Well, that was okay, I thought. Much better than the treadmill. I had something other than myself in a mirror to look at as I ran. I had people to dodge on pavements, and it didn't quite feel like time had stopped still while I ran my twenty minutes. I like this. So, I did it again. And again. And for the next two years, that was my run. I didn't explore side streets. I never turned right. I knew this route was 20 minutes, and that was all I needed.

When I moved to a new house and started living in the south side of Glasgow, I found a new route. This time I turned right from Langside to Newlands, turned right again at Giffnock and then right at Shawlands to get back to my flat. Sometimes I would run it faster. Sometimes I would run it slower. But I would never turn left and run into Queens Park, even though my flat overlooked it, and it has, I now know, a great 5km loop. Once I found a loop, I stuck with it.

It was only a few years later that I turned left. It wasn't deliberate. It just happened. I'd started running my regular route from the flat when Scottish Water had set up a diversion and blocked access to a bridge five minutes into the run. I had no choice. Instead of turning right, I had to turn left.

In my head, I was grumbling. All my thoughts of where to run have been blocked. How could I run four miles if I couldn't run the first mile? Where would I go?

But, as I ran, a thought took hold. Why not turn left again? Why not try and run randomly? Every time I would get to a junction, I would ask myself, "Which road do I know the least?" and that's the way I'd go.

In the process, I discovered a new trial, a new park, and a new interest in running. I wasn't running; I was exploring. And I hadn't realised that running was more than just exercise. It wasn't just 20 minutes of moving arms and legs; it was also a chance to discover new places.

While there's joy in running the same routes, the comfort of knowing where you're going, what you'll see and the calmness that comes from not thinking about anything at all, there's no spark: the same roads, the same streets, the same pavements, the same beat. No one ever said, "Do you know what I find fun? Doing the same thing as yesterday and the day before and the year before that."

I decided then I would always 'turn left' just as long as it was not the same way I'd always gone before. And while there was fear of getting lost or finding a route that was worse than the one you'd planned, that's a pessimistic view. You might discover crocodiles, mud, or, worse, a long straight road (is there anything more boring than not turning?). You might also find a hill with an escalator - I can but a dream.

And while the university may have introduced me to running, it also introduced me to routines and not looking for the edge because, when you only turn right, you're just running in circles. So instead, I tried to do more, even if I didn't know what that was.

Iain

I left university without a degree... because I accidentally left my degree under my chair at my graduation.

My graduation year was 1999. During the ceremony, I was told that all the names of everyone graduating would be immortalised on a wall to celebrate the fact we were the last graduates of the 20th century. I've been back to the university many times since then. But, unfortunately, I've never found the wall.

It's probably a toilet block somewhere.

What I took from university was more important than a bit of paper or a name on a wall. I learnt to trust my instinct. Why do anything just because someone tells you to do it? Think for yourself and do what you want.

Andrew, a lawyer

Which is good advice for life, and very bad advice if stopped by the cops.

PART 2

CHAPTER FOUR: SWIMMING

Iain

After leaving university, my first job was for an internet company called Madasafish. Yes, that is the real name. Madasafish supplied internet access and webspace to customers in the UK. It was during the early 2000s, and all internet companies tended to have memorable names.

One of my tasks was to track down users who had done something terrible online. Which sounds like a great job: I would be an internet vigilante. I thought I would be tracking down terrorists, criminals, or gangsters, but it mainly dealt with far worse people than that - lawyers.

Andrew, still a lawyer

Objection, my lord!

Iain

The most frequent request would come from the lawyers of 20th Century Fox, the TV show The Simpsons owner, asking that I remove pictures of their characters that users had uploaded to our webspace without permission. Homer Simpson might act stupid, but he is very well informed about copyright infringement.

Occasionally I would receive a more exciting request. One time I received an email from NASA asking me to track down a user who had tried to hack their servers.

I tracked down the culprit. I phoned them. A man answered. I confirmed they were the person I was after and then explained they were in serious trouble. NASA was threatening to report them to the police. The man burst into tears and screamed, "MUM!!! I don't want to go to jail."

I had forgotten to check the age of the man I phoned. He wasn't a man; he was a 12-year-old boy. His mum came on the phone and shouted at me for making her son cry.

Eventually, I was promoted from this role. I passed the task of hunting down Simpson fans to another man. I explained how to do it:

- Get the IP address of the user

- Get the time and date they were online

- Run a script using that will return the username of the user.

- Check the username in the database to get their address and telephone number

- Contact the user.

- Tell them to stop it (whatever it was they were accused of doing)

I showed him how to do the task. Then, I got him to do it again. I got him to do the steps repeatedly until he knew exactly how to do it.

The day after showing and explaining the steps to him, there was a request from a lawyer. I asked the other man to look at it.

He said, "What do I do with it?"

I replied, "The task I showed you how to do yesterday."

He looked at me blankly. "What task?"

He had forgotten all the steps I had shown him the previous day.

Which is a valuable lesson: doing the same thing, again and again, is not learning. If you do not understand what you are doing, then repeating a task won't make you any better at it.

This is why swimming is a skill, not a sport. You can get better at a sport by putting in more effort. For example, running is a sport; if you want to run faster, move your legs faster. BUT if you're going to swim faster, you cannot just swing your arms faster. You must learn to swing them correctly. Otherwise, you will keep making the same mistake again and again but more often.

Concentrate on the how and why of swimming, and you will swim faster, quicker, and more efficiently.

It took me 20 years to learn this.

Andrew

Ignoring Iain's comments about lawyers. Unlike people who work in IT, all fine upstanding people who just happen to spend all day constantly closing their browser when anyone walks by as they are looking at the sites that are banned to everyone else in the office.

Instead, let's talk about someone else. A true hero. Ross Edgeley, who in November 2018 became the first person to swim around mainland Great Britain.

Six months later, I watched him on stage talking about his amazing feat and his not so amazing feet. The constant swimming and lack of walking had destroyed the skin of his feet, so it looked like he had jellyfish for soles.

He also revealed that exposure to saltwater during the swim had destroyed his tongue. So it was no wonder it had taken six months to speak about his achievement as, I imagine, he had to wait for his tongue to grow back.

Over the two hours of the talk, he passed on some of the lessons he learned. The one tip that stayed with me was this one.

"Be naïve enough to start and stubborn enough to finish."

Iain

I started to swim in the 1980s. My Dad taught me using the "do not drown" approach.

He made me stand two metres from a pool wall. I then tried to swim to the wall. If I did not drown, he would increase my swim to three metres from the wall, four metres etc.

My fear of drowning meant I quickly learnt to swim. Unfortunately, my Dad only knew the breaststroke, so that was all I learnt. He did not see the point in freestyle swimming. His view was, "Why do you want to stick your head under the water? There is nothing to see here except people's feet."

My school attempted to teach me other strokes, but I was not very good at them. In addition, I hated the weekly swimming lesson at our local leisure centre. I found the smell of chlorine in the pool overbearing.

I have subsequently discovered chlorine has no smell. The smell in the pool was from chloramines, which build up in pool water when the water is not properly clean. A smelly pool is an unclean pool.

If I had known that, I would have hated swimming even more than I did.

Andrew

I don't remember drowning. Maybe I was a natural, and the whole learning to swim lessons didn't leave any lasting memories. I can remember swimming, but I can't remember learning to swim. Instead, I remember trunks and towels.

We would swim on holiday in the small Perthshire town of Aberfeldy. It has a sports centre with a 25-metre pool and every day on holiday we would go for a swim. But, first, we would get ready by grabbing our towel, folding it lengthwise in half and then rolling it up with our trunks inside. We'd then carry it under our arm up to the centre. We'd then unroll it, get changed and then repeat on the way home – except this time our armpits would get wet because we're carrying a soggy towel and trunks.

We never thought to use a bag. There was no need, and once a towel was rolled up with your trunks, then you didn't need anything else. Not even goggles because, for some reason, our Dad didn't believe in goggles. "You don't need them", he'd say, "If you duck your head under the water, it'll sting for a minute, but you'll soon adjust."

Which was okay for him to say as he only had one good eye. His other eye was damaged due to an operation in his thirties to cure an aneurysm. It was an operation that was so medically advanced he spent the rest of his life with doctors saying, "I've never seen that before".

He would start swimming without googles and then say, "you'll get used to it".

We didn't.

I could never put my head under the water. I still struggle when water gets into my goggles. I need to stop and clear it.

But I never got goggles. It never occurred to me. I was learning from my Dad, so I just did what he did. Even if he was a medical miracle, who thought he was Aquaman and I was a boy scared of getting his head wet.

Iain

My first ever open water swim occurred during my school years. My class went away for a weekend to an outdoor centre by the Atlantic Ocean.

For some reason, which I cannot remember, the teacher made us stand on a pier next to the sea. I had to strip to my swim shorts and then jump in the sea. It was November. The water was freezing. I nearly drowned. As soon as I divided into the cold water, my body seized up, and I struggled to breathe.

Imagine the scandal now if a teacher forced a class to jump into the Atlantic in November without checking if the pupils could swim. It would be a scandal. Back then, it was known as 'building character'.

Andrew

It wasn't just the Atlantic where we learnt to swim. Teachers would try and teach us different strokes at the local pool as part of our PE lessons. But yet again, no one thought to use goggles. We'd try and learn how to swim the crawl (it was never called freestyle), and we'd have to duck our heads under the water, which, with no goggles, was a disaster. Imagine 30 kids all trying to swim from one side of a pool to another. All arms were flailing, all legs akimbo. All with their eyes firmly shut and swimming right into each other. Every lesson would end when one kid knocked another kid out, accidentally headbutting them while swimming with their eyes shut. It would be 20 years before I tried the crawl again, afraid that I would only end up with a concussion again if I did.

Swimming outdoors was no more attractive. Our aunt Margaret hired a caravan on Coll beach, just outside of Stornoway and near our granny's house one summer. It was a typical Lewis summer. Grey sky. Cold wind. Rain likely. Perfect weather to go paddling in the sea. We lasted 30 seconds.

I'd brought my trunks to the caravan, wrapped in a towel, of course. We changed there and ran down to the water's edge. By the time we got there, we'd invented Avatar, 25 years before James Cameron had thought of his race of blue-skinned people. The water was even colder.

"Aaaaaaaarrrrrrrrrrggghh!"

We ran back to the caravan.

And that was my outdoor swimming experience. One dip.

Barely up to the waist. And that was it.

Today, people say it's invigorating. Soul clearing. But when you're ten years old, the only thought you have, when the waves reach your crotch, is "Eeeeeeeek! I can't feel my balls!"

I didn't venture back to the sea until I was 25. I was on holiday in the United States. I stayed near the oldest town in the United States, Augustine, which was settled in the 1500s then comprehensively rebuilt to be a Walt Disney version of a historic town. So if you like your McDonald drive-thrus to be housed in a replica Spanish villa that looks like a Spanish conquistador just built it, then Augustine is the place for you.

I had a motel beside a beach, and I decided it would be fun to swim in the sea, despite the fact I'd not swum since school, and I didn't have any trunks or, naturally, any goggles.

"It'll be okay," I thought, "I'll soon get used to it".

Waves were crashing on the shore as I waded out. The water was warm, which was the first shock. Could water be warm? Could the ocean be a bath? The second shock was when I ducked under a wave. Salt. What the effing eff was salty water doing to my eye. It was like Tom Cruise had taken my acid eyeball bath and placed it in a mixer with a cheese grater and was recreating his finest tricks and flicks from Cocktail.

Disorientated, eye shut, frantically trying to clear the water from them, I swam out further and further until I thought I should turn back. Except I couldn't.

I couldn't understand it. The waves were going towards the shore. They were big and powerful and heading in the direction I wanted to go, but why, when I swam towards the shore, was I not going forward?

I tried to swim faster by kicking harder; the only way I knew how to swim faster was because my arms were as good to me when swimming as Douglas Bader's legs.

I went backwards.

Damn.

I thought of shouting; however, there were some people on-shore, and I had another idea. There were surfers up the beach. They were further out, but they were making it back in. And the only difference between them and me was that they had aboard. So, I should pretend to be a surfboard, and I'll surf back in. Genius.

Next wave. I lay as stiff as I could and kicked forward just as the crest of the wave passed through me. I did the same again with the next wave and the next until I reached the shore, thankful and ecstatic that I'd discovered the secret to not drowning. Don't swim. You can't drown if you stay on the beach.

So, I didn't swim again. At least, not for another ten years. And during those ten years, I can confirm that I didn't drown once.

Iain

I didn't discover a love of swimming until I joined the Arlington bath club. – the oldest surviving Victorian bathing complex in the world. It didn't have a small verruca puddle, and it didn't stink of chlorine

I joined for one reason – I was dating a girl, and she swam there every day. So I thought it would help me woo her if I joined too.

She invited me to a swim session. There was just one problem. I'd recently shaved my legs. I'd read that it would help my cycling by making me more aerodynamic. What it didn't mention was that it would make me look like a freaky hairless legged twat.

I'm glad to say it didn't put her off. She is now my wife.

She is an excellent swimmer. I was terrible. All I could swim was the heads-up breaststroke. I did one lap, and she turned around and said, "What is it with your weird kicky out leg action?"

I didn't know I had a weird kicky out leg action. So this was news to me.

She started to show me some simple moves to improve my swimming.

Despite joining the pool, I hardly saw her. She liked to swim at 7 am. I prefer swimming at 7 pm.

I told her, "you will never see me here at 7 am. You will never see me do front crawl. I just like a wee swim to relax".

Within a week, I was annoyed that she was fast and good at swimming. So I started learning the front crawl.

Within three months, I was swimming at 7 am. And she was swimming at 7 pm. It turned out she wasn't swimming first thing in the morning because she loved getting up early; she just didn't want to be seen with a man whose legs were smoother than a tadpole.

Andrew

One month later, he was teaching me to swim. I thought he knew what he was doing. He thought he knew what he was doing. We were both wrong.

I hadn't swum at all since Florida. However, I had recently decided to combine my love of running and cycling into a new challenge – the Henley Half, a middle-distance triathlon with a 1.9km swim in the River Thames.

I was inspired to do it by a BBC show about comedian David Walliams and his attempt to swim across the English Channel.

I thought if David Walliams can swim the channel, and he's just a comedian, not a sportsman, then I can swim too. So, when Iain said he'd started swimming at the Arlington, I decided to join him. I even bought a pair of swim goggles.

My first lesson can be summed up by the phrase "It's all about the breathing,"

Iain said this repeatedly, but he didn't explain how this advice differed from, you know, the general advice for everyone on this planet in how to live. Breathe. Yes, that's the easy part – but how do you do it underwater?

But, perseverance led me to eventually swim 100m without stopping. Four laps. I was happy with my achievement until I discovered the Arlington swimming pool had borrowed its tape measure from the PE department of the Nicolson Institute, and the pool was only 21 metres long. So, I hadn't swum 100 metres at all. Instead, I'd swam 84m.

Iain

I soon realised the only way to get better at swimming is to be coached.

Andrew

By a proper coach. Not Iain.

Iain

I discovered my local triathlon club, Glasgow Triathlon Club, had a Sunday night swimming session for beginners.

I thought it would be a welcoming environment full of like-minded beginners. It wasn't. Triathletes lie about their ability, and they are competitive.

I discovered this when the coach said: "I'd like you all to swim eight lengths of the pool at 70% race pace. I'll time you. Who wants to go first?"

No one volunteered to go first.

"Come on! Who's fastest?"

Everyone looked at each other in the same way a lift of strangers looked at each other after one person had farted. Who was it?

I looked at the man next to me. He was solid muscle. His

back had the classic v-profile of an Olympic swimmer. He wore tiny Speedos that were so small and revealing they looked like they'd been tattooed to his crotch. His swim goggles cost more than my last car.

"Hurry up! Someone has to go first!"

The only time I'd been mistaken for a swimmer was when a hairdresser said to me, "Are you a swimmer?" I beamed with pride and replied "yes," thinking it was because of my swimmer's physique – but my pride was quickly punctured when the hairdresser said, "I thought so – I examined your hair. It is in terrible condition. It is dry from chlorine."

I did not even have the right equipment for a swim. My swim shorts were run shorts. There was no point buying one pair for running and one for swimming. It meant my run shorts got a wash. My goggles were whatever I could find in the lost and of found bucket of my local pool. I was not a swimmer.

He looked at me again. It wasn't that he was in a different league to me: we weren't even playing the same sport.

He said: "You first, mate."

I replied, "No thanks. You should go first."

He thought about it and said, "no – I think you are quicker."

So, I went first. I had a five-second head start. Then, on the sixth second, he caught up.

I went as fast as I could, but he kept having to stop to wait for me.

After we'd finished eight laps, the coach said, "are you all happy with your time?"

The man who couldn't have been more like a fish even if he'd had gills said, "I could have gone faster, but I got held up". Maybe if he hadn't lied about his ability, he wouldn't have gotten held up.

If you are good at something, it's okay to say you are good at it.

I then looked around and saw everyone else. It was like the scene at the start of Saving Private Ryan. Bodies were strewn in the water. People were screaming in agony. One man looked like he'd swum himself into a heart attack.

The coach asked, "Was that 70% effort?" No-one replied. They were all completely knackered.

At last, the man having the heart attack said through wheezy, non-competitive gasps of death, "I think I went 65%".

Andrew

Before lockdown, I would try to train at a weekly swim session with Glasgow Triathlon Club at 7 am on a Wednesday. I say "try to train" because there are only eight places and the online booking system was more popular than free Ice Cream in a desert. The places filled up within minutes of opening. It got to the stage where you needed to camp out overnight if you wanted a spot.

Who knew a 7 am spot would be so popular? But, despite the early start to get there, it was a great session as, for the first time, I was swimming to a coached session rather than swimming back and forth until I got bored.

Swimming is my least favourite sport. I enjoy it but, given a choice between running or cycling or smelling of chlorine, I will choose not to smell of a chemical.

During an average session, I would swim between 1.5km to 2km, which is more than I would swim independently. So, as a good way of swimming longer, it's good to join a coached session. But, on the downside, I also found out that everything I was doing was wrong. Wrong hands, wrong arms, wrong legs.

For the first few weeks, I had to relearn how to swim. I need to pat the water, not karate, chop the water with my hands. I need to stretch my arms out like I'm celebrating, not bring them in like I'm about to fall asleep on them. Legs need to kick more. Hips need to turn. I need to 'push' the water back, not flail my arms like a helicopter. And I have to get up at 6 am to get there.

It took six months before the coach stopped asking me to change my stroke or the position of my head, or the way I kick my legs. This just goes to show, even the best coaches will eventually give up.

Iain

After many months of training, I decided to enter a swim race. It was a sea swim at Elie Beach in Fife. It was a charity event that was advertised as a one-mile swim in a flat calm bay. Unfortunately for me, the remnants of a Caribbean hurricane had raced across the Atlantic just in time for the swim start.

The wind was fierce. It was so strong the Woman's Open Golf Championship at nearby St Andrews cancelled the days play because of fears for the safety of fans and players.

Upon hearing that the golf was cancelled, I fully expected my sea swim to be cancelled too. However, if it was too unsafe to be on land, it was too risky to be off it.

The event was not cancelled.

I stood on the beach, hopping until the last moment, the organisers would see sense and postpone the swim. They didn't see sense. Finally, a whistle was blown, and the swim began.

I ran into the water and immediately ran back out again. Unfortunately, I'd forgotten my goggles.

I put on goggles. I ran back into the water and tried to swim freestyle. I lasted one stroke before a huge wave smashed into the side of my head, knocking my goggles off. I hadn't put them on correctly.

I tightened my goggles and started swimming again, but a wave struck me in the face whilst my mouth was open. Unlike Monika Lewinsky, I swallowed. I spluttered to a stop as my lungs filled with seawater.

I composed myself and decided to do the only thing I could think of to get through it. I changed to breaststroke so I could keep my head up and see the waves coming. I could then take evasive action and duck under the wave before they hit me.

I was supposed to swim out to a buoy, but I decided to cut the swim short. It was too far and too dangerous for me to reach. I managed to do a few hundred metres, but it felt a lot more.

The organisers marked me as a DNF, but I'd argue my swim was a success. It was an achievement to get in the water and survive. The distance swam was irrelevant. The bright point is that since this race, I've not feared bad conditions because every swim since seems gentle compared to that one.

Andrew

Before my first open water swim, I was told I should splash my forehead with water so that I'd know how cold it was going to be.

This seemed like terrible advice. The last thing I want to do before swimming in open water is to splash my forehead with water because... it's BLOODY FREEZING!!!

In Scotland, if you're going for a dip, you need balls of steel – and toes of steel and feet of steel and basically, an entire body made from a metal that doesn't feel the cold.

But the thing is, you adjust to it. The more you do it, the easier it gets. The more you swim outside. The more your body adjusts to the temperature until eventually your skinny dipping in Ben & Jerry's and wondering why it's so warm.

But first, I had to get in. So, I splashed my forehead with water and got in the water. It was freezing. And it was fantastic. And one day, I might have the feeling in my feet back.

Iain

At my current workplace, I sit next to a Dutchman. On Friday, he asked me what my plans for the weekend were. I told him I was going to a Wim Hof Method workshop.

Wim is also Dutch. His nickname is The Iceman because of his ability to endure cold conditions. He has swum under the North Pole ice, can sit in ice baths for 90 minutes, and ran a marathon in the Arctic Circle shirtless and shoeless. So I assumed he must be very famous in Holland.

My colleague looked at me and said, "Wim, who????"

Wim needs to work harder on his Dutch PR.

My colleague then asked what the Wim Hof Method is?

"If I knew what his method was, I wouldn't be going on the course!" I replied.

#spoileralert (Don't read on if you don't want the method spoiled)

The method has three pillars

Cold therapy – Wim claims that exposure to the cold starts a cascade of health benefits such as improving your immune system and helping with fat loss. It will also encourage the production of endorphins— the feel-good chemicals in the brain that naturally elevate your mood.

Breathing – Wim claims that improving your breathing will release more energy, reduce stress levels, and help your immune system.

Commitment – Wim claims both cold exposure and breathing require patience and dedication to be fully mastered. Only through practice can the other two benefit you.

It was a great class, but it's not rocket science. Remember to breathe properly before and during your time in the water.

Breathing wasn't as easy I thought it was going to be. First, I learnt that I shallow breathe a lot. I don't take deep breaths to the back of my lungs.

I wasn't the only person who struggled with breathing. When told to breath calmly and gently, one man exhaled his breath so violently through his nose it was like a volcanic eruption of snot and air.

Despite the instructor reminding everyone to breathe calmly, the volcano continued his enthusiastic eruptions. I think he was trying to impress his partner, who was also attending the course. Like a gorilla in the jungle marking their territory by huffing, puffing, and bashing their chest, he was making sure she knew he was the manliest breather in the room.

When it came to the swimming part of the course, we had to jump into the North Sea in just our shorts. Unsurprisingly, Wim Kong – the breathing gorilla was the first person to jump in. I hope, like a gorilla, he didn't piss in the water to mark his territory.

Andrew

Iain might get swim survival tips from Wim, but I get mine 90s sitcom Friends.

There are not many 90s sitcoms that you can turn to for survival tips. Frasier could help you charm a maître-d. For example, Only Fools & Horses would warn you about the dangerous lack of arm support whilst leaning on a bar top. But only Friends could help you in the wild, and by wild, I mean beach.

In Friends, six friends, hence the title of the programme, in case you've not seen it, go to the beach. One of the friends is stung by a jellyfish, and another of the friends suggests they, ahem, relieve themselves on the spot where it stings as, ahem, urine, ahem, is a cure for jellyfish stings...

Now, you have to ask yourself how this cure was first discovered. Who's first thought was, "I know, let's piss on it".

And, having found success in combatting jellyfish, did they try and expand?

"I have a headache. Does anyone have any aspirin?"

"No need, I know what to do – let's stand on a chair and piss on your head!"

"I've broken my leg; can someone call an ambulance?"

"Save yourself a phone call – I've got a better idea – let's piss on it".

In Friends, that's exactly what they do. They piss on the friend with the jellyfish sting, and, lo and behold; the friend is cured. Or at least I think that's what happens. I've not seen this episode in years, so I can't say that there is an episode of Friends where five friends form a circle and piss on the sixth. I can imagine that happening in Seinfeld, but somehow it doesn't seem right for Friends. Perhaps they all did it into a cup, and then it was poured on delicately.

Anyways, whether circle pished or applied from a potty pot, that episode of Friends stuck in my mind, and I've always known what to do when a jellyfish stings. Fortunately, I've never had to put this into practice, as I've never been stung by a jellyfish until I was swimming off South Beach in Miami.

I didn't need the Wim Hoff technique. Instead, I had sun loungers, cocktails and warm water.

I'd only swam a short distance when I felt small electric shocks along my arm. I knew I was stung, but I wasn't sure by what. I could feel itchiness and knew I had to swim back to shore and speak to the lifeguard, but all I could think was, "Is he going to piss on it?"

I'd seen Friends, and I knew what happened next.

I climbed the lifeguards' tower, showed him my arm, now turning blotchy red, and said, "I think I've been stung."

He said, "It's a jellyfish; let me get something for that."

And he grabbed a bottle.

While part of me thought how good it was that he prepared for this emergency by bottling himself in advance, another part of me thought, "Please let it be something else. Please let it be anything else".

"It's vinegar," he said, spraying the liquid on my outstretched arm.

I sniffed.

It was vinegar.

Vinegar is a cure for jellyfish.

When I swim somewhere with jellyfish, I always bring a special water bottle to help with the transition. I also bring a bottle of Saxo vinegar – filled with pish.

Iain

I've had some memorable experiences outdoor swimming. Although not always related to the swim. My favourite spot to go to is North Third Reservoir near Stirling. The reservoir is strangely named as I can find no record of a North First or North Second Reservoir. Maybe this one was the third time lucky after the other two failed.

The reservoir is a great spot for swimming. The reservoir has high cliffs on one side, which form a dramatic backdrop. The surrounding area is forested with bike and walking trails. It's a nature lovers paradise, but it's also a paradise for lovers of a different kind.

"A MAN found lying on a rug wearing only "frilly woman's underpants" at a beauty spot near Stirling was found guilty of public indecency" was the headline of a story in The Daily Record in 2017

"Brian Bone (50) was lying down on a rock wearing nothing but the pants near the North Third reservoir."

Stirling Sheriff Court heard last Thursday how police found the delivery driver at a particularly popular spot for "gay cruising", but Bone said that he was only there because it was his favourite place for sunbathing.

But Bone denied in evidence there was any sexual motive to his behaviour.

He said: "I had been sunbathing there for about two years.

"I had extensive building work done in my garden, so I found it much nicer to head up there because it was nice and quiet.

"There was nothing sexual about me going there, though. I would just go up for a couple of hours and sunbathe on my own.

"My wife is fine with it too, and she'd make me sandwiches and cola for my afternoons up there."

He added: "I'd brought my rug to lie on, but I'd forgotten my shorts. So I was wearing just my boxers so I could get a good tan when the police arrived.

"I was in the process of urinating when I heard footsteps and ran back to my rug. I panicked. That was the reason I was exposed."

The police asked him if he was gay or bisexual but said he was confused about what to say because he didn't know what bisexual meant.

My favourite bit of the story is his very British excuse – "I can't possibly be having sex with men. My wife made me sandwiches".

I don't think I helped the reservoir's reputation. A van of men pulled up at the car park just after I changed into my wetsuit. They looked at me like I was a weirdo. I think they thought I was wearing a gimp outfit.

I wanted to take a photo before I swam. I spotted a good spot to take it from – a bridge over the river leading to the loch. Unfortunately, the entrance to the bridge was blocked off. There was a sign on it that read "Condemned – do not cross." I thought about it for a second and then decided to ignore it. What was the worst thing that could happen?

The bridge had slats missing, so I had to be careful as I walked across to not fall through the gaps. Finally, I reached the halfway point successfully. I took a photo, turned around and took a step forward. I'd forgotten to look where I was going. My foot landed in one of the gaps in the bridge, and my leg fell through it.

I took a hefty knock to my thigh, but as I fell, I did have the wherewithal to place my camera down gently on a slat rather than see it fall into the river. I was impressed with my quick thinking to ensure my picture would survive even if I did not.

I managed to get back to my feet, and thankfully the only thing that hurt was my pride. I managed to swim around one of the reservoir's islands. I'd highly recommend it as a swimming spot. Just remember to bring sandwiches.

Andrew

Swimming doesn't have to take place in the great outdoors. It can be done in our cities too. For example, London has the Serpentine.

Whenever I go to London, I always like to try something new. The last time I visited, I tried modern opera* and swimming in the Serpentine.

First, I had to buy a towel as I'd forgotten to bring one. The Serpentine is in Knightsbridge. There are no cheap towel shops in Knightsbridge. It looked like I was faced with either buying a monographed gold set from Harrods or the finest designer ostrich feather towel from Harvey Nicholls. Luckily, I spotted a Laura Ashley with a 50% off sign and managed to get one there. Even that was a struggle.

"I'd like to buy a towel, please," I said to the assistant

"What kind of towel are you looking for," they asked.

"The cheapest," I said

They gave me a look which said, "Knightsbridge is not for you, sir".

The Serpentine Lido is an old white building with a marked 30 metre by 100-metre bay at the edge of the Serpentine lake. While the changing rooms were small – only two changing booths – the Lido was clean and the staff pleasant.

Three women were leaving the Lido as I walked towards it. They saw me in my trunks. They said, "you must be brave". I assume they meant swimming in the cold water and not because I was wearing trunks aged over 40.

With no one else in the pond, I had the Serpentine to myself. Except for a few swans. And the lifeguard, who thought he was going to get to go back inside when the women got out of the water and were annoyed, he had to stay when I came in. But knowing there was someone watching was reassuring in case the Swans decided to attack.

If you're in London, I'd recommend a trip to the Lido. It was fun to swim in the middle of Hyde Park, and, with the pool to myself, it was quite a change from the crowds around Harrods.

*P.s. I cannot recommend modern opera. The singing was good, and I got caught up a few times in the music, but the lyrics were awful. Or at least the lyrics as translated and projected above the stage as surtitles.

At one point, the hero, a man in love with a woman, spent 10 minutes singing about "the oxen in the field are looking strong", "tonight's a good night to pick strawberries", and "this is not the time for my plough to break" while the woman he was in love with repeatedly sang "I'm not as black as you think I am – it's just the light!".

Farming and mild racism.

That's modern opera.

It wasn't for me.

Iain

One time I went swimming at Balgray Reservoir. A spot I'd never been to before. I was standing half-naked in the car park next to the reservoir when a man approached me and said.

"Is this where the group meets for swimming?"

I was not part of a group and did not know what he was asking about, so I replied, "Sorry, I'm not part of a group."

He looked confused by my answer. But I realised he was probably confused about why I would be half-naked, trying to get one leg in a wetsuit, if I wasn't part of the swimming group.

To put his confused mind at rest, I added. "I'm swimming too, but just not with a group."

He didn't go away. He waited a minute and then said, "is it an 800m loop?"

"Is what an 800m loop?" I asked.

"The swim?" He replied.

"I don't know. I'm not with the group!" I was starting to get annoyed.

He waited a minute and then said, "Are you in charge of the group?"

"NO!!! I'm not in the group! I'm just trying to go for a swim!"

He looked like he finally realised I could not help him, but it did not stop him from asking one final question.

"How much is it to join?"

Andrew

Last year I went on a train from Glasgow Central to London with Iain.

"Have you got the tickets?" I asked.

Usually, that is an innocuous question, but we were standing on the train, and it was pulling out of Glasgow Central. It was too late to hear no for an answer as I did not have them.

"No," he said, "you've got them".

Which I sort of did but mainly did not. Because, while I had them on my phone with all details teasingly shown on my Trainline app, it was just a reservation and not the tickets themselves. The tickets were still sitting unprinted in the ticket machine at Central Station.

I could have cried. But, critically, I didn't because I'm a man, and men don't cry. Not unless they've just read "A Boy in The Water".

"A Boy in The Water" by Tom Gregory tells how he became the youngest person to swim on the English Channel. It's no spoiler to confirm he succeeds because, unlike most sports biographies, this one doesn't rely on peril.

Instead, A Boy in The Water deals with trust and faith between a boy, Tom Gregory, and his coach as he's pushed to swim further and further. And it's this trust which provides the tension because it's never clear how much of the goal was driven by the boy or the coach and whether it was right for an 11-year-old to even attempt such a swim.

Written from a child's perspective, the book is simple and straightforward, with the relationship explored through a back and forth between the swim itself and the three years of training leading up to it. Training sessions in Dover Harbour, solo swims across Lake Windermere, and a sense of sporting success achieved through coffee mornings, battered vans and digestive biscuits as treats. And minimal discussion of swimming.

No passages describe swimming strokes or the goals of any training sessions, just brief, powerful descriptions of the swimmers, the coaches and the music listened to on home-made mix-tapes. And an ending, which managed to show how powerful trust and faith and belief can be and what happens when they're gone.

For me, the joy of swimming isn't about strokes or times. It is about the bond of doing something with Iain. And a reminder that you should always swim with someone and never swim on your own.

Iain

Swimming is not a sport. It is medicine. No matter how I feel before I swim, I always come out mentally and physically refreshed.

CHAPTER FIVE:
BIKING

Iain

If you look up the Wikipedia entry of any professional cyclist, you will find a section devoted to a rider's palmarès. This is their list of achievements, accomplishments or wins. For example, Chris Froome has listed his achievements as:

- 4x GC Tour de France ('17, '16, '15, '13)

- 3x GC Critérium du Dauphiné ('16, '15, '13)

- 2x GC Vuelta a España ('17, '11)

- 7x Stage Tour de France ('16, '15, '13, '12)

My Palmares is quite different. It has:

- 1 x Cycling Proficiency Badge ('85)

I have never won a race or even come close to winning a race. Yet, it is claimed God loves a trier. Well, he must love me. I've tried and tried.

My first bike race was the Bealach Na Ba sportive in the North West of Scotland. This race boasts the greatest ascent of any road in the UK: it begins at sea level and rises to a height of 626m. It takes six miles to get from sea level to the top.

The name Bealach na Ba means 'pass of the cattle.' It was initially a gravel track used by crofters to move cattle between two parts of the Applecross peninsula. It's now used mainly by tourists. The route is part of the famous North Coast 500, now known as one of the top coastal road trips in the world.

Recently the route nearly changed its name due to a copyright claim by my mum's favourite shop – Marks and Spencer's. Lawyers for M&S intervened when a group tried to trademark the route to produce branded merchandise such as hoodies, T-shirts and baseball caps.

M&S raised concern over a potential trademark infringement concerning North Coast, the retailer's in-house clothing brand, which it claims "mixes rugged casualwear with relaxed styling for an easy, laid-back look". Which means it makes clothes un-fashionable dads wear.

M&S closed their clothing brand shortly after, and the lawsuit came to nothing.

The race launched in 2006. I remember reading about it in the Herald newspaper. I had passed by that part of the Highlands many times when commuting between the mainland and my parents in Stornoway, but I never knew the climb existed. So I entered the second edition in 2007.

At the start line, I looked at the other riders.

They are all using road bikes; I'm on a mountain bike. I'm the only one on a mountain bike. Why are they not on Mountain bikes? We are going to ride up a mountain. Surely a mountain bike is the most effective way to do it?

They are all wearing skin-tight lycra. I am wearing a thick win-ter jacket and a pair of baggy shorts.

They are all clipped into their bike using proper bike shoes. I'm wearing trainers.

They all have a bottle on their bike. I do not have a bottle on my bike. Instead, I have a backpack containing a sandwich, a two-litre bottle of water, and a map in case I get lost.

It is fair to say; I do not know what I am doing.

Andrew is here, but he is not riding. He offered to drive a van around the course in case I needed him. I spot my friend Malcolm who is also doing the race. I say to him, "Good luck." He says, "You'll need it more than me", and he then rides off. All the other bikes whizz past me.

I now realise why they are on road bikes. Honestly, up until this point, I thought there was no difference between a road bike and a mountain bike. I had assumed road bikes did not go up hills.

After two hours of cycling, I'd cycled further than I ever have before. However, I realise it is two hours back to where I started, so I will need to do the same again to get home.

I stopped and ate a sandwich. I wonder how the other cyclists are getting on. They must be starving. They don't have any sandwiches.

I try phoning Andrew, but I don't get a signal. The race is too remote for mobiles to work correctly.

After another hour of cycling, I reach the start of the climb. The sign at the bottom says: "Road to Applecross (Bealach Na BA). This road rises to a height of 2053ft with gradients of 1 in 5 and hairpin bends. NOT ADVISED FOR LEARNER DRIVERS, VERY LARGE VEHICLES OR CARAVANS AFTER FIRST MILE."

It does not mention bikes. That means I will have to do it.

I start the climb. Within 100 metres, I start to sweat. I take off my jacket; I put it in my backpack; I restart the climb. It doesn't feel too harsh yet.

The road gets steeper. I try to switch to a lower gear - I am already in my lowest gear. No wonder the start was easy.

The road climbs higher. I struggle to turn my pedals. I haven't even done one mile of the climb. I'm still at the part safe for learner drivers, huge vehicles, and caravans.

Maybe a bit of food will help. I stop and eat the rest of my sandwich.

I restart the climb. I feel heavy. The sandwich has not helped. I struggle onwards. I stand up on the pedals to make them turn. I stop and admire the view. I consider quitting. I don't have to think twice. I decide to quit.

I wish I could say I have the stomach to battle it out when things get hard, but I don't. I try phoning Andrew again. He can come and rescue me. There is still no reception. Feck. I'll have to keep going. Mainly because I assume I'll get phone reception at the top of the hill.

I push my bike to the top of the hill. A film crew is waiting for me. Probably not me specifically but for anyone doing the race. They are filming for BBC Two Scotland's The Adventure Show. The reporter approaches me: "I can't believe you're using a mountain bike."

"It's my only bike," I admit.

I take out my water bottle to have a swig.

"You carried that up the mountain?"

"Yes," I said, "I thought I'd get thirsty."

"You do know the organisers supply water and food at regular stops?"

I thought I had to supply everything myself. Doh!

I tried my mobile. It has a signal. I try Andrew, but there is no answer. I sent him a text saying. "I quit! Come and get me at the bottom of the hill in Applecross."

The descent of the other side is great fun — six miles of fast downhill with treacherous corners. At one corner, an ambulance is tending to a rider. I think to myself how glad I am that it is not me.

At the bottom of the hill, I reach Andrew. There are 40 miles to go, but I'm not doing any more. I'd achieved my race by cycling further and higher than ever before.

We head to the finish to wait for Malcolm... and wait... and wait... and we....

As it gets dark, there's no sign of Malcolm. I approach the race organisers and ask if they have seen him. They go to check their list of riders. When they come back, they have bad news – Malcolm was the man I passed on the mountain who was getting tended to by the ambulance.

The news got worse. He was taken to hospital. I assume they mean a hospital in Inverness, the nearest city, but the news is even worse. The hospital is not Inverness, which is close by and on our way home. He has been sent to Broadfoot on the Isle of Skye, which is miles away and nowhere near our route home.

We head to Skye to collect him. He is sitting on a chair with his arm in a sling. His brakes failed whilst taking a corner on the descent. The bad news was he broke his collarbone and will be off work for six weeks. The good news is that he can use his good arm for drinking a pint.

The next day at work, everyone asks how I got on at the race. I tell them about Malcolm. No one questions whether I finished. They all assume I did. I do not correct them. Was that a lie? Technically, nobody asked; I did not tell, but I should have admitted that I did not finish.

Bealach na Ba was my first bike race and my first bike DNF.

Andrew

To be fair to Iain, that's the only time he's failed to complete a bike race in Scotland. Note that I'm saying "in Scotland". We'll get to foreign jaunts later. Before that, it's worth jumping forward a few years to the time I asked him: "When's the worst time to get a puncture – the start or end of a race?"

In 2015, we were about five miles from the finish of Bealach Beag – a shorter 45-mile race around Applecross - when we passed a rider changing a tyre at the side of the road.

"If you get a puncture at the start, then that's annoying as you've just started, and you have to stop. But, if you get a puncture at the end, you think that you don't have long to go when, suddenly, you've got to wait and change your tyre."

Iain didn't answer the question. Finally, we came to a short hill, fast descent and sudden climb. I'd read the course profile and knew that the last two miles were downhill. I thought if I made a break for it now, then Iain wouldn't keep up.

I was right. I was first over the hill. I kept going as fast as I could for two miles, looked back and knew he wasn't in sight. It was an easy victory.

Until I had to wait at the finish line.

And wait.

And wait some more.

Eventually, 20 minutes later, far, far longer than he should have been, Iain cycles into Sheildag.

"I got a puncture just after you left".

He tried to claim that meant my victory was void, that professionals who get a mechanical in the last stage of a race are given the same time as the winner.

I pointed out that I was the first to climb Bealach Na Ba. And that some parts have a gradient of 20% – which is almost like doing a wheelie without your bike leaving the ground.

I also pointed out that I was the first round Applecross and had waited for him. But still, he insisted he was given the same time.

So, I said: "That's okay, you can have the same time – but you don't see Chris Froome handing over the yellow jersey. It's the same time, not the same podium place! I'm still the winner".

Which is the kind of logic you need when you have a winning streak to defend. A winning streak that started during another race: the Caledonian Etape.

Iain

"Dear Steven Spielberg." I wrote.

"I know you're busy, but I have reserved you one ticket for my acting debut on Thursday night. Harrison Ford is getting a bit old for Indiana Jones, so you might want to cast a younger, more Scottish actor. I can supply my own whip and hat! If you can't make it can you pass this onto Martin Scorsese"

That was my Facebook status update on June 10th 2010. I had completed an evening course called "Learn to Act", and that night I was due to give my first ever acting performance in a scene involving a serial killer and the landlady of bed and breakfast. I was the serial killer. The acting tutor said I was per-fect for the part. I am not sure that was a compliment.

The other actor was an older woman. The first thing she asked me at rehearsal was: "What accent are you going to use?"

"My own," I replied, "but louder so the people at the back can hear me."

The performance went well. I was myself but louder, and she performed the scene with a perfect Yorkshire accent.

Afterwards, the tutor said to her: "You were amazing. You transformed yourself and inhibited that character. As a result, you could easily work in theatre."

He then turned to me as said: "As long as you enjoyed yourself."

I did enjoy myself, but I never acted again. I thought about con-tinuing. I could have gone onto the next level of the course. But I know my limitations and accepted that I would never have the talent, desire, or range of accents to be good at acting. So, just like Bealach na Ba, I stopped at my top.

I hadn't entered a bike race since Bealach na Ba until I read about the Etape Caledonia. It is an 81-mile closed road sportive in Perthshire, one of Scotland largest bike races, with over 3,000 riders taking part each year. However, it's not a race. The organisers make that very clear – it's a sportive, which is French for "we get cheap insurance If we don't call this a race".

The race passes by the town of Aberfeldy. My great grandfather comes from Aberfeldy. He worked for a local landowner and had four daughters. The daughters were expected to work for the landowner too, but they wanted to get proper jobs.

The landowner was furious about this and thought they had ideas above their station. So they were sacked and made homeless. My Gran went to Glasgow. One daughter stayed on in Aberfeldy, and the other two went to Edinburgh and London.

Every year Gran would take her family (including my Dad) to Aberfeldy for a summer holiday. My Dad did the same with our family.

It felt appropriate that as my first race was the one closest to my home, my second race should be closest to another home – my holiday home.

I'm not the only person who likes going to Aberfeldy for a holiday. Harry Potter author J K Rowling has a holiday home on the outskirts of town. Usually, it's a quiet location, but her house is on the route of the Etape. Five thousand cyclists pass the entrance and probably don't realise who lives in it. But one year, instead of whizzing by JK Rowling's home, I whizzed on her home. It is not one of my proudest moments - I did a wee in her driveway. Which I think was okay because she wasn't at home. A feeble excuse, but I was desperate, and her driveway was a convenient spot to stop.

A few years later, I was at an event that she attended. I was introduced to her. I should have said, "Hi there, I really enjoy your books," but instead, I said, "Hi there, I pished on your gate."

I then told her that she could use it in Harry Potter and the Search for a Toilet. A book where Harry Potter has one too many Butter Beers and then tries to make it home. She looked impressed but, so far, she has not written the book yet. Maybe I have confused impressed with appalled. The only way the conversation could go worse is if I'd mentioned that whilst I was on her driveway, gripping my wand, I shouted, "Expelliarmus!!!!"

I honestly cannot remember anything about the actual race. I think I did it on my mountain bike, and I'm pretty sure I finished near last.

I am also confident it rained. It has rained at least once during every Etape that I have done.

The Caledonian Etape has become the annual test of Todd v Todd as I try (and fail) to claim the triple crowns of Todd Of The Loch (the fastest Todd around Loch Tummel), Todd of The Mountain (the fastest Todd up the highest climb at Schiehallion) and, the big one, the Yellow Todd, the fastest Todd overall and first over the finish line.

Andrew

I'm not sure about the title of "Yellow Todd", it sounds like either I have a severe liver problem, or I ran away from the convoy when the injuns came to town in an old fashioned western.

"Who's that at the bar by himself?"

"That be Yellow Todd, a craven and a coward!"

But since neither of us speaks French, officially, as both of us achieved the lowest possible mark, it's possible to succeed at secondary school French, a mark so low that my teacher's main criticism of me was: "You couldn't even pronounce the English words right," Yellow Todd it is, and not the more exotic-sounding Jaune Todd. But, of course, when you say it, it does sound like John Todd, and John is the English version of Iain, so perhaps it's with some irony that I talk about the Todd Championships and a jersey named after Iain but one he rarely wins.

Competition is important. It started in school with the somewhat healthier competition of academic achievement. Who could win the most prizes at the end of year prize giving?

One year, I won two – English and Technical Studies. Afterwards, walking along a corridor, a teacher stopped me and said, "Congratulations on your award."

"Awards," I said, holding up two certificates because I was an arrogant wee prick.

I don't remember Iain winning any awards, but really, who remembers losers? I bet James Cameron, after winning umpteen Oscars for Titanic, couldn't name another nominee. He didn't need to. He was King of the World.

Our sporting rivalry didn't start until university. Iain played squash because he went to Edinburgh, and that was the kind of thing you did in Edinburgh while waiting for your turn to play croquet on the lawn.

We had two squash courts in Stornoway, both in a single building with a shared balcony where people could watch. As the balcony stretched across both courts, it meant that anything said on one court could be heard on the other, which was okay for the first five minutes. And then Iain would claim a ball was out, or below the line, or I'd blocked his shot or any of many other minor rules he claimed I'd broken. After 10 minutes, he would introduce random swear words to emphasise how strongly he felt about me breaking the rules. Then I'd introduce a few more, then voices would rise, racquets would be gripped with white knuckles, and the next disputed point would lead to shouting so loud you could hear it on the mainland and not just the balcony or the court next door. After a few months, we had to abandon our games after one angry father barged onto the court and told us exactly what he thought about our language and the words his two young sons could hear. An argument validly made but undermined as he used swearwords even we didn't know.

Iain

I decided to do Bealach na Ba again. But this time, I trained for the race, wore the correct cycling kit, and bought a new hybrid bike. It was a mix of a road and mountain bike. Surely that would be perfect for climbing hills on roads.

At registration, I had to complete a release form stating I absolved the organisers of any blame in the event of an accident. I assume this was due to Malcolm's misfortune, as they did not ask this last time.

I lined up at the start. I felt confident. I turned to Andrew and told him that: "I think it is going to be a great day." I spoke too soon. It started raining.

This time the climb was much more manageable. I made it halfway up before I had to get off and push my bike. There was no camera crew at the top this year. There was no one at the top. The conditions were miserable – wet and windy. Nobody wanted to hang about in that type of weather.

I was pleased when I biked past Applecross. The climb was done. The rest of the course would be easy…

It wasn't. The miles after Applecross are an endlessly undulating series of small hills. There was more climbing in this section than the Bealach climb.

By the time I hit the umpteenth small hill, I had to get off and push my bike. My legs had run out of puff.

Andrew was on a road bike. He felt fine. Maybe when Lance Armstrong was wrong when he wrote, "It's not about the bike." This was definitely all about the bike.

I made it to the second last village on the route: Shieldaig. It's a small coastal town. The organisers had set up a feed stop here. They were packing it away into a van. They looked surprised to see us. A man approached and said, "I didn't realise anyone was still biking".

I assume that means we are last. Very last. He opened his van and said, "Help yourself to anything you want".

I took a packet of crisps, a can of coke and some cheese slices. I'd never seen cheese at a food stop before.

I tried a bit. It was delicious. It was the best bit of cheese I have ever had. It was probably the cheapest cheese imaginable, but after cycling 60 miles, my taste buds must have craved the milk and salty goodness. I've never had cheese as good as that again. To this day, I still drool at the tastiness of that cheese.

Powered up on the three C's - cheese, coke and crisps - we head off to tackle the last section of the course.

It was horrific. For the last 12 miles, we had to ride into a strong headwind. I had to stand up on my pedals to move my bike forwards. It was like biking through heavy mud.

At last, we spotted the finish. It was getting dark. We had been riding for nearly nine hours. I was spent but elated. Finally, we were going to finish. We had done it together. Then, with 100 metres to go, Andrew sprinted off. He did not believe in doing it together. He believed in winning. He was the only one at the finish line when I got there. Everyone else had gone home.

We drove home. He spent the five-hour journey telling me how he was the winner of the Bealach na Todd.

Andrew

Which is a good name. I don't remember it being 100 metres to go. I think it was more like five miles to go. I thought I would put my head down and would keep cycling hard until the finish.

85

Technically, I was second last in the race, but I was also first Todd. So that makes 'a winner' if not 'the winner'.

Iain

I once took part in a go-kart race. Before I started, the marshal gave a safety briefing. He explained that if he waved a black flag, that was a warning that I was driving beyond my ability. If he waved it again, then I would be disqualified.

I got in the kart and waited for the green light to flash

RED..........wait.....wait......GREEN!

My kart accelerated from the start line. I was immediately in the lead, but a car was coming up quickly on my outside right. We both approached the first corner, a tight left-hand turn.

It looked like he was able to turn left before me. I should have slowed down, but instead, I accelerated and slammed into the side of the other car. This pushed him off the track but allowed me to take the left turn. A masterful bit of driving, but the marshal black-flagged me for driving beyond my ability.

A couple of minutes later, I received a second black flag for a manoeuvre that wouldn't have been out of place in a Mad Max film. I was disqualified.

I could not understand what I had done wrong. I should have been praised. Driving beyond my ability is surely a compliment, isn't it?

Did Schumacher win all his Grand Prix's by driving within his ability? No – he went to the limit and beyond.

I was thinking about this as I drove home from the go-kart track...in an AA van. I was so pumped up with adrenaline from karting I'd crashed my car after leaving the track. I had to phone the AA to get me home.

The AA man asked how I'd crashed. I replied, "I was driving beyond my ability."

Fleetwood Mac singer Christine McVie was asked by Rolling Stone magazine to reflect on making the album Mirage. She said, "I don't think any of us remember a huge amount about it. But I don't remember there being anything bad about it; how about that?"

This sums up my next attempt at the Etape Caledonia in 2012. Unfortunately, I don't remember anything about it other than I don't think anything wrong happened. The reason I don't know is that we had a new goal - L'Etape du Tour.

L'Etape du Tour is a French race, which allows cyclists to ride a stage of the Tour de France on closed roads on the same route as the riders of the official race.

It was a 197KM stage from Pau to Bagnères de Luchon. The route encompassed five climbs comprising 4000m of elevation, including the Col d'Aubisque and Col du Tourmalet. These climbs have featured regularly in the Tour De France. A challenging stage that would challenge the world's best cyclists.

Once I signed up for the race, I told everyone what I was doing. I told all my friends, all my workmates, I even told total strangers. This would be the biggest event of my life. It was not just a race. It was a defining moment of who I am. I was no longer Iain who had failed to do Bealach Na Ba and had come near last at the Caledonia Etape. I was now a Tour De France cyclist in training.

I did not realise at the time that I was defining myself by something I was going to do rather than by something I had done. My self-worth was now entwined in this potential achievement. Which was okay if I achieved my goal, but what would happen if I did not?

I did not own a road bike, so my first step was to buy one. It was my first ever road bike. I did not check out what gears it had – or even attempt to ride it beforehand. Instead, I bought it because I liked the colour. I am sure Chris Froome used a similar principle when he headed to the Tour.

I knew very little about the route other than the course profile map showed two Haute Categories (HC) climbs and two Cat 1 climbs. I did not understand what HC meant, but I now know HC means "holy crap – how can this road keep going up?"

In the six months before the race, I trained harder than I had ever trained before, which was nowhere near enough.

Before I left to go to France, my workmates and friends all wished me luck. They said they would check the leader board to see how I got on. I told them to check from last place to first place. That way, they would find my name quicker.

I was unprepared for the race. I did not even own proper cycling clothing. Instead, I wore a regular t-shirt, a pair of shorts, and I brought along a Gore-Tex jacket that I used for hillwalking just in case it rained.

The day before the race was beautifully sunny, but the forecast for race day was grim - rain and wind. This slightly reassured me. At least the condition would recreate what I was used to at home in Scotland.

We headed to the start at 0600. Unfortunately, I got a puncture on the way to the start line. This day was not going to go well. I hoped for the best but expected the worst.

The race began at 0700. To stagger the number of riders on the course, the riders are grouped into pens of 200 riders. Each pen is released every couple of minutes after the start. The organisers encourage the slower riders to seed themselves in the pens that leave last. So we self-seeded ourselves in the last pen to leave.

To complete the course, a minimum speed of 14mph is required. If I went slower than 14mph, a sweeper bus would catch up, and I would have to get off my bike and get on the bus.

Choosing to start last was a mistake. The sweeper bus left as soon as the last pen left. Our pen - the slowest riders, the ones who needed the most time, were the ones who get the least time.

Disaster struck as I crossed the start line – my pump fell off my bike. I had to stop and go back for it. The sweeper bus waited as I picked it up. I was nearly swept up before I had even got going. I restarted and crossed the start line successfully.

It was 36 kilometres to the base of the first serious challenge of the day, the Col d'Aubisque.

For the first 4km, the gradient is gentle. After that, I allowed my legs to get used to the rigours of climbing 1,190 metres of elevation.

Although it had been dry at the start of the race, the rain began when the road started to rear up a 13 per cent section towards the Cascade de Valentin. According to the race guide, there would be "little time to draw breath and enjoy the stunning mountain scenery."

There was no mountain scenery. The rain and cloud meant there was very little visibility. I could see a couple of hundred metres up the road, but that was as good as it got

It took me nearly two hours to do the climb. It takes Tour De France riders 40 minutes. Due to the visibility, I did not realise I was at the top. Supposedly, there is a sign - three giant steel bikes individually painted in yellow, green and polka-dot colours, but I must have missed them amongst the fog and rain.

The ride down the hill was torture. It was an hour of freewheeling downhill cycling. Occasionally I would brake if it felt I was going too fast to take a corner. I had never freewheeled for such a long distance. Also, the lack of movement in my body meant I was freezing.

There was no time for a rest at the bottom. I had to start the long climb of Tourmalet. Unfortunately, the sweeper wagon was not far behind me. For a couple of miles, I managed to stay ahead of it. Although I could see it looming closer and closer every time, I looked behind me.

Eventually, it caught me. I had to get off my bike and get on the bus.

I could accept getting on the bus. However, I was not fit enough or good enough to get any further.

It didn't affect me until I went home. All the people I told I was doing it asked how I had on. I had to say to them I had DNF'd. I was no longer Iain, the Tour de France cyclist. I was Iain the failure.

Andrew

I don't look at it as a failure. Failure suggests there was a chance of success. We were never going to be successful because we had no idea what we were trying to do. You might as well ask your pet cat to round up sheep or ask Gerard Butler to use any accent other than his own. We didn't plan, and we certainly didn't think the race through – my only thought was, "Dougie, did this so we can do it too".

Don't worry if you don't know Dougie; I didn't either. He was a guy I worked with on a university project when I was studying for an MBA in 2009 and 2010. He spotted me cycling into the university one day and told me that he was also a cyclist. What I didn't know at the time was that this was the equivalent of me driving into the university in my small cream coloured Fiat 500 and then bumping into Lewis Hamilton, who says, "I like to drive too".

I found out later that Dougie used to take one-way train trips to England just to jump out at Carlisle or further so he could then cycle home. On his way home from work, he would cycle 50 miles or more on a mid-week night. I thought I was at the same level even though I only cycled for 15 minutes to get home from work.

During one class, he told me that he'd taken part in a race that allowed you to ride the route as the professionals in the Tour de France. I thought it sounded brilliant and immediately checked out how to apply. But, unfortunately, I didn't check out the route or work out how high an actual Alp was. I thought it was a hill, not a mountain, and no higher than some of the hills around Glasgow. And even when I checked the elevation and saw that we would be climbing higher than Ben Nevis, I still had no idea how high that would be because I'd never climbed Ben Nevis.

Ignorance is bliss – until you find yourself climbing an Alp for 10 miles and expecting it to take 20 minutes only to see you're still climbing two hours later. Ignorance wasn't bliss; it was stupidity. On the slope of the Tourmalet, the end couldn't come fast enough.

Iain

To get better, we needed to improve – and the fastest way to do that, we thought, was to join a gym.

Andrew and I were both members of the same gym. It was a corporate shed in a posh suburb of Glasgow. The people who went were so rich the car park looked like a Range Rover showroom.

The gym had every facility two 'world-class cyclists' could need – state of a art gym, state of the art weights and a state-of-the-art pool. Everything was state of the art, except the art – that came from Ikea.

Unfortunately, the only thing we were world-class at was our ability to use a jacuzzi back then.

Some people say there's nothing better than jumping in a jacuzzi after a hard gym session. They're wrong. It's even better if you've not used the gym. Why work up a sweat and get tired when you could have spent that time floating in soapy bubbles?

We'd head in and spend ten minutes in the Jacuzzi, but then we'd get out and get in the other Jacuzzi. Yes – this gym was so posh it had two Jacuzzis. At least we got some exercise walking between the two.

We didn't just use the two Jacuzzis. We'd often get out and head to the pool - and then past the pool to the sauna. The sauna in any Glasgow gym is predominately a male environment. I've often thought the main reason women pay so much for a spa is to avoid sauna-ing with men.

This sauna never had any women, but it did have three bald men. Sometimes just one of them, sometimes two but often all three. We called them the "Baldy Men Club."

A sauna is relatively small, and we could hear their conversation. However, they only had one topic – themselves. Namely, how well they had used the gym before getting to the sauna.

Week after week. We'd listen as each tried to out-compete each other. "I just did 10K on the running machine in 30 minutes", One would say. Another would reply, "Did you bike 20K first? I always bike first and then run". The third man would try to beat this and add: "Did I mention I bench pressed three times my body weight today, and I didn't even sweat once?" Which should have led to a trip to see a doctor and not the Jacuzzi.

We talked about the Baldy Men Club and their strange ways until we realised they probably talked about us – "Can you believe how much nonsense they talk? One of them claims he's done a stage of the Tour De France, but the only exercise I've seen him do is dry himself with a towel after the jacuzzi".

To beat Andrew, I decided to do double sessions. So, I joined another gym too. I work for a university, and I can access the onsite gym there. It was cheap, but it had a significant downside. I've seen all my workmates naked. Not in a creepy, hiding up a tree with binoculars type of way but in a let's all get naked in a shower way. That sounds just as creepy as the tree.

Until recently, the male locker room had a communal shower. In the ten years, I've gone there, I've seen a lot of naked men. It's fair to say I've seen all members of staff and all staff's members.

One time I went to use the shower but realised I had no towel to dry myself. My options were:

1. Don't shower. I ruled this out because I had a meeting to attend, and I couldn't turn up looking like the cat had dragged in.

2. Use my t-shirt to dry myself. I ruled this out as my t-shirt was soaked through with sweat, so I'd end up just as dirty as I was before I'd showered.

3. Use the hand dryer.

This is why many naked men and students looked on as a naked 6ft man tried to get his body underneath the hand dryer. Do you know how hard it was to dry my back using a hand drier? It's hard. The blower kept switching off as the angle of my back couldn't keep the infra-red beam on.

Since that day, my workmates have looked at me with new-found respect because not only had they seen me naked. They've seen me naked limbo-ing under a hand drier. That takes real skill.

Andrew

I have seen nakedness in the gym too. I was in a sauna when all I could see was another man's knackers.

It was difficult to avoid them. They were staring me in the face. It was surprising to see them because, well, I was sitting in the middle of a sauna at the Sir Chirs Hoy Velodrome that was:

A.   Open to men and woman; and

B.   Not a nudist beach.

"Hello," said the knackers. Or the man. It was difficult to know where to look. Knackers or man. Man or knackers.

"Hello," I said, wondering if I should say something like, "PUT SOME CLOTHES ON!"

"It's nice here," he said.

"It is," I said, again wondering if I should say something like, "PUT SOME CLOTHES ON NOW!!!"

"I've never been here before," he said.

Clearly not.

He then sat up.

I should mention that throughout this entire conversation, he'd been lying down, stretched out on his back on a raised wooden bench that encircled the sauna, while I'd just sat down on a lower bench and had turned my head and gazed straight into his knackers.

Sitting up didn't improve anything. Now everything dangled.

And still, he acted like it was perfectly normal to be sitting in the nude in the middle of a sauna open to all. And still, I didn't tell him to put some clothes on because, well, I was just trying to be polite. I should have left. But there are strict rules about leaving saunas or steam rules. You can't leave as soon as you get in because you're then showing that you don't like the people already there while you can't go when someone else comes in because that saying you don't like the person who's just arrived.

There is only a tiny window of opportunity to enter and leave a sauna without offending anyone else.

Also, don't get me started with the awkwardness of sitting in a sauna when someone of the opposite sex comes in and you're the only person there. Do you stay, but that might make them uncomfortable in a sauna with a stranger? Or do you leave, but then that might make them think you're going because you don't like them?

It's a minefield.

That's why it's best just to sit. Even if the person you're sitting next to has their crown jewels on display. It's just polite to stay.

But still. If you are going to a sauna, can you please keep your clothes on?

Iain

The following year I was due to take part in both Etape's again, but I came down with flu just before the Etape Caledonia. Not the regular flu but life-threatening man flu.

My fellow men will sympathise at just how potent this horrific affliction can be. Its only known cure is watching TV, drinking beer, and replying, "no, I'm ill" to any enquiries about whether any housework is going to be done.

Unfortunately, it meant I did not get to take part in the race. I went to the sauna instead.

Thankfully that was only my B race for the year. My A race was a second attempt at the L'Etape du Tour. But, this time, I did not tell anyone I was doing it.

I didn't tell anyone because I wanted to do this race for myself, not for the glory of showing off to others.

Andrew was using his bike for the race, but I decided to hire one, so I paid for one ride only like a pauper at a whorehouse. This was the first time I rode a carbon road bike.

The stage was a loop starting and ending in the Beautiful French town of Annecy. It had never been used as a Tour de France stage before, so there was very little information about the route. However, I assumed it would be similar to the previous one with lots of ups and downs.

The initial section was flat and easy as we rode alongside Lake Annecy. The weather was nice and sunny, so we made good progress. The first climb was a steady incline, but we felt good as we reached the summit of Col de Leschaux.

After this point, the road widened, so we rode side by side. Occasionally Andrew would drop behind me. I didn't worry about it as he would appear again a few minutes later, but just before the next climb, Andrew dropped back and then didn't reappear.

I stopped and waited. Hundreds of riders passed me, but there was no sign of Andrew.

Eventually, he turned up. His gears were broken. The chain was consistently slipping off. I tried to fix it, but the problem persisted. Finally, someone else stopped to help, but they couldn't fix it either.

Andrew decided to wait for a motorbike mechanic. I offered to stay, but he encouraged me to carry on. I left him by the side of the road. I expected he'd catch up with me later in the race.

The race was hard. The first two climbs had barely any shade from the hot sun. I was going as fast as I could on one climb, but I still got passed by a Frenchman wearing sandals on a bike with a basket full of his shopping.

The last climb was brutal. Riders were lying by the side of the road, exhausted by the warm weather. Nevertheless, I was determined to finish, so I vowed not to stop. I knew I'd never start up again.

I expected a glorious finish, but it was pretty disappointing. I crossed the line. A man gave me a small cheap looking medal and then told me to clear off as there was no room on top for people to hang around.

I was in and out of the finish line in seconds. There was no time to savour the achievement.

Andrew was waiting for me when I got back to our hotel. His race had ended due to his mechanical problem. The mechanic had been unable to resolve it.

If every cloud has a silver lining, then Andrew's should have been getting back in enough time to see Andy Murray play the Wimbledon final. The first time a British man had won Wimbledon in years.

Unfortunately, his cloud had no silver lining. His cloud had thunderbolts and lightning. The hotel wasn't showing the tennis. Andrew had to sit bored out of his mind watching French TV whilst he waited for me.

Andrew

I was fully fit for the Etape Caledonia, but the weather forecast for the race was terrible. Every motorway sign on the way to the race warned of "Heavy Rain"; however, every time I looked up, it was blue sky. I checked the forecast, and the rain wasn't starting until 7 am the next day. I was due to begin at 6:55 am.

That night, before the race, I stayed in a small inn about half an hour away from the start. I ordered haggis because I'm Scottish, and, yes, we do eat it at times other than a Burns Supper. I like haggis because it's mince in a sock. However, despite being Scottish, I draw the line at a deep-fried Mars bar. I'd sooner eat a sock.

During the race, I discovered a new tactic for dealing with heavy rain. While it felt like I was taking part in the America's Cup as rain and spray combined to form a continuous rolling tsunami of water, I found that it would ease if I tucked in behind another rider. And not just a couple of metres behind, politely hang back so as not to be too apparent that you're using them as a rain break. But right on their wheel. So, close their doctor would say, "You'll need to take a step back if you're going to examine their prostate." And what I found, as I moved from wheel to wheel, is that the bigger the arse, the bigger the protection. If only Cardi B was a cyclist and rode amateur races in conditions that would cause Noah to retreat to his woodshed. Sadly, she wasn't. I imagine, with thighs that big, she was more of a track cyclist. So, my tactics consisted of finding the most

97

oversized arses in the peloton and sticking to them as close as a human centipede.

It was ideal preparation for the Etape Du Tour because I was ready to make full use of the sweeping chains of bikes that would drag me around, and I would be ideally placed to join any mini pelotons that would form because (a) it was France; and (b) in my mildly racist ways I thought that's what the French do, isn't it? Form pelotons. And wear onions round their neck.

Alas, as Iain has said, my race ended faster than you peel an onion. One small climb. One descent. One puncture. One spin of the front wheel. One eye-catching three-inch tear in a tyre wall. One attempt to flag down a Mavic mechanic on a bright yellow motorbike and one "Sorry, we've run out of tyres". The only lucky thing to happen was that I was only a few minutes from a checkpoint, so I didn't have to push my bike far to find some water, an energy bar and then a short wait before getting picked up by the sweeper bus. DNF? I'm not sure I can even say I started.

After that I swore, I wouldn't enter any foreign races again. It was too risky and too expensive to travel so far, only for something random to end it – even if I did get a medal. Iain nicked one at the end and brought it back to the hotel. I'm ashamed to say I still have it.

Iain

The following year, 2014, I needed a new bike to commute to work, so I went to a bike shop to buy one. I spoke to the shop assistant and asked, "I'd like to buy a bike to commute to work."

He replied, "What type of bike are you looking for?"

I thought about what I would like, and I decided, "I'd like a bike which is so boring, nobody would ever want to steal it."

He pointed at a boring looking bike. "I have just the bike for you," The bike had no distinguishing features and no expensive parts. I thought nobody would steal it until the day someone did.

I had been cautious when I parked the bike. I had made sure I locked it and that it was in front of a security camera.

That did not prevent someone from stealing it. I asked the buildings security team to review the security camera footage, but it only revealed a family of spiders had taken up home in the camera casing. In addition, they had spun a web, which obscured the security cameras view of my bike.

I scoured Facebook/gumtree/2nd hand shops for the next week, but I did not find the bike anywhere. I assumed I would never see it again, but six months later, I spotted my bike chained to a bike rack.

It could not be my bike. Could it?

I checked the bike thoroughly. It looked the same. It had the same mudguards, the same scratch mark on the frame, and the same pedals mine had.

It was my bike.

I called the police and asked them what to do. They sent two officers who waited at the bike for the thief to return.

A few hours later, I got a call asking me to come back to the bike. When I got there, they were standing with a man who looked similar to me. He had the same colour hair and the same type of glasses as I had. The man said the bike was his.

The police checked his story, and it turned out he more than looked like me. He also worked at a university, just as I did. He had bought the bike on the cycle scheme. Just like I had. He had bought it from the same bike shop as I had, and he added the same mudguards and bike pedals.

However, he couldn't have had the same scratch like me, could he?!

Yes, he could. The scratch mark across the frame was a design flaw on the bike. All the models of these bikes had the same scratch. But unlike me, he had a serial number for the bike so the bike shop could confirm it was his.

He was my bike twin. The only thing that differentiated us was temperament. I am very easygoing and rarely argue. However, he got furious and shouted at everyone for wasting his time.

He biked off. I secretly hoped he would get a puncture on the way home. He was an arse. And not one of the good ones who keep you dry in the rain. One of the arsey arses also describes what I thought of Andrew at that year's Etape Caledonia. We agreed at the start that if we got separated during the race, we'd meet at the next food stop on the course. The race started. He immediately biked off. I didn't worry about it because I knew I'd get him at the next food stop. I arrived at the food stop and he was nowhere to be seen. I waited 10 minutes, he didn't turn up, and I realised I'd been tricked. He went on to win the race easily because he didn't stop once.

Andrew

To be fair, I did want to win. However, it wasn't deliberate, at least not at first.

The first food stop was around 20 miles from the start. We never stop there as we've had something to eat at the start, and it's okay to cycle through to the second stop before needing to refill water bottles. So, I wasn't expecting Iain to be there. I thought he would be cycling slower for me to catch up. It was a mistake until I didn't stop.

I admit I could have stopped. By the time we were getting to the second stop, I had thought he must be behind but, there was still a doubt in mind that he might have stabbed me in the back like pop star Olly Murs ditching his duties as best man for his own twin brother's wedding to attend an X-factor rehearsal. Iain could have been my Olly, ditching me for his shot at stardom. It turned out that I was Olly, and he was the twin left behind. But that's not my fault, and it's his. He could have done it to me; first, the fact he didn't doesn't excuse him from possibly doing it, even though he hadn't. Anyway, I won, and my winning streak of Caledonian Etape races became more than just a "oh, Andrew won"; it started to become a psychological block. I could see it in his eyes. A nervous twitch whenever the Etape was mentioned. The occasional lapse into silent contemplation when the defeats played heavy on his mind. I think 2014 was the year that I broke Iain. Or was it the year he broke himself? He could have won but chose not to. That's a heavy burden to bear, even if he did do the nice thing and wait.

But before you start thinking that he's a nice guy, also know that it's the year that he swore to get revenge. And no one nice ever vows to get revenge. You don't hear of people turning up to their mum's house on Mother's Day with a surprise revenge. Or families reunited live on television after years of living apart only for one to turn to the other and say, "now, I will get my revenge".

This was the year that Iain changed. No longer Mr Nice Guy. He swore that next year would be different. And it was. He lost in entirely different circumstances.

Iain

I knew I had to change. If the measure of failure is to do the same thing and get the same result repeatedly, I needed to change what I was doing. If I couldn't win outdoors, then I needed to win indoors. So, we signed up for track cycling at Glasgow's Sir Chris Hoy velodrome. A four-session training programme that would give us the right to cycle the track anytime. The first three-session were straightforward, but on the fourth:

"This is not a race, do not treat it as a race. There will be no winners or losers. Are we clear about that?"

I was with a group of about twenty people. We were doing the "Introduction to Track Cycling" course at Glasgow velodrome. The man giving the instruction was the track cycling coach.

"Get on your bikes and do not race; I'm judging you on your ability to ride safely, not quickly."

We were all ready to start. One of the other riders was in a complete cycling club team kit. Even his socks were branded with the name of his cycling club. He wore sunglasses indoors. He looked like a twat.

"Are we ready to start?" Asked the coach.

A man suddenly appeared next to twattymactwatface. He wore full cycling kit too. He turned to his identical twat and said: "You can win this."

No – you can't. It's not a race. Did you not hear what the coach just said?

He started giving Luke Twatwalker a pep talk: "Take it easy on the first lap and then use your power on the second. Don't be afraid to cut people up."

No – don't cut people up. Take it easy on the first lap and then even easier on the second. Demonstrate you can do this safely.

He then added "F**k them up" and slapped Encyclopaedia Twatanica on the back.

IT'S NOT A RACE! NO ONE IS GETTING F**KED UP!

The 'not a race' started. Everyone set off at a steady pace except Lance Twatstrong: he shot off. I could hear him mutter: "You can do this".

There's nothing to do: it's not a race. It's a bunch of middle-aged men living out a Chris Hoy fantasy. We just want to spin about a bit and then go home for tea.

His mate started shouting, "YES! You're at the front. Keep it up".

Twatasuarous Tex soon caught up with me. We were both about to reach the tiered banking. He pulled out wide to go around me, but he was going too fast and couldn't control his bike. He hit the top of the track. His bike slipped, and he came off. I looked up. The bike and the rider were now sliding down the banking towards me. I did what any man would do in this situation. I closed my eyes and hoped for the best. Track bikes have no brakes, and even if they did, I couldn't use them on the banking. I had no way of avoiding being hit.

His bike went through mine. I fell off. I hit my head on the wooded boards of the banking and scraped the skin off my arm and shoulder.

The coach came running over. He took one look at the two of us and asked, "Are you okay?" My head hurt, and I had a bit of skin rash from the slide but nothing serious. Twatzilla looked surprisingly chipper, all considering. We both said, "I think so...."

The coach thought for a second and said, "Thank f**k for that. Now imagine how sore it would have been if you'd been racing".

I've never been back to the velodrome since that day.

I hoped that training at the velodrome would aid my chances of beating Andrew at the Etape Caledonia, but after my accident, I decided on a different path. If you can't win fair and square, then cheat. But, unfortunately, I faint at the sight of blood and needles, so doping was out as an option.

So instead, I decided to use my mind and outthink Andrew.

I told him, "I've got a secret weapon to beat you at this year's race."

I didn't have one.

I just told him that to make him paranoid. I hoped the energy he would waste trying to figure out how I would beat him would tire him out.

Except he outthought me. He brought a ringer to the race. A man capable of biking very fast. Andrew knew my weakness at bike races. I hate riding behind other cyclists. I consider it cheating. I'd rather bike out in front all by myself than sit behind someone else.

Where's the achievement in drafting? Who wants to be the best at hiding in a pack?

When watching bike races, I admire the riders who burst off the front in futile efforts to breakaways. To me, that is actual cycling.

The race started. Andrew immediately drafted his ringer. They both raced off. I didn't see either again until the end. What a flippin' cheat.

Andrew

Iain tried mind games before the race.

"I've got a secret weapon," he said.

"What is it?" I asked.

"If I told you, it wouldn't be a secret, would it?"

"If you're secret doesn't involve pedalling faster, then it's not going to help".

But he had me worried. He was cycling far more than me. I've had to rely more on Turbo sessions than cycling outdoors. So, I thought there was a good chance he would win this year. I didn't tell him that; instead, I said:

"I don't have a secret weapon. I'm going to tell you exactly what I'm going to do. I'm going to sit behind you until the very last mile; then I'm going to overtake you."

And every time he mentioned his secret weapon, I'd tell him the same thing except...

... I wasn't going to do that at all. Instead, I planned to take a break as soon as the course flattened out around the 30-mile point at Loch Tummel.

In French, they call this Le Mind Game. I think. Did I mention I failed my French standard grade?

And I had a backup. I knew another rider who was starting in the same wave as us. Someone I knew was fast and completed it in just over four hours last time they raced the Etape. I made sure we met him at the start, and I then stuck to his wheel for the beginning of the race.

I had a domestique, which is French for 'I Ain't Going to Lose This, So I Got Some Secret Help to Get Around'.

And the plan worked to perfection. We stuck together for the first 15 miles along a gentle rolling road towards Kinloch Rannoch before 'dropping' Iain just before the first feed stop.

Dropping is English for "See Ya Later, Loser!".

After that, I wanted to see how fast I could go. I had it in my head that I might, with a fair wind, be able to beat four hours. But, in the end, my legs gave up before I did. There are two main climbs during the Etape. The first is at Schiehallion, a steady climb with some steep corners that shock the system after 40 miles of flat roads; the second is three miles from the end, a very steep climb of fewer than 100 metres. My legs threw in the towel on the second climb and, after that, I knew my faint hope of getting in below four hours was over. Nevertheless, I coasted the last few miles and rolled into Pitlochry for a time of four hours six minutes.

I then waited for Iain.

And waited.

And waited.

Maybe next year would be different?

Iain

This isn't the first book Andrew, and I have written. During the Scottish Independence referendum, we wrote a parody of the SNP's white paper. It was called The Fat Ministers Question Time. It had a few good jokes and a lot of bad ones, but it made fun of everyone equally.

Some people didn't get the joke. One man wrote a review that said

"This book is an insult to the democratically elected Scottish government, but it's surprisingly good value for money."

I'm glad he could see value for money even if he couldn't see any value in the jokes.

Because independence wasn't a divisive topic, we next tackled football and wrote a book that made fun of Glasgow Celtic and Ranger but mostly Rangers. It was written with love, so we were never mean, and we didn't once tackle any of the religious sides of the clubs. That was a topic not worth joking about.

It also attracted reviews like

"This is the least funny book I have ever read, but at least it was only a pound."

Hopefully, even if you hate this book, you'll at least appreciate how well priced it is.

One of the hardest parts of the Etape Caledonia is getting reasonable value accommodation that it is close enough to the start that we don't have to get up too early to drive to the start line.

This year we lucked out. Andrew had a friend who'd bought a B&B near the start. We are very easy guests as we don't have many requirements other than location.

For example, my breakfast conversation goes typically.

B+B Owner: What time do you want breakfast? 5 am?

Me: It's okay. I don't like a cooked breakfast. If you leave out cereal and milk, then I'll have that.

B+B Owner: Are you sure? How about tea and coffee?

Me: No thanks. You don't need to get up. The cereal will be great.

B+B Owner: If it's not an issue....

Me: Thanks. I'll be happy with the cereal. Enjoy your lie in.

When I get home, I rate the B+B on TripAdvisor. "1 star – No cooked breakfast."

If that review were accurate (the story is, but the review isn't), then you'd read that review and think the B&B was terrible. The review is a snapshot, but it's not the whole story.

Similarly, a picture at a race is a snapshot that doesn't give the whole story. If you saw a photo of both of us at the end of the race, you would think we both looked fit and happy. It doesn't show that we both had a heavy cold, but at least I'd made it to the start line this year.

Andrew dropped me at mile 20. I tried to catch up, but my chest would seize up when I pushed hard, and I'd have to cough.

I accepted it wasn't going to be my day. The rest of the race was spent at a steady non-coughing pace. I finished with a personal best, so I can't complain.... too much.

The next day I felt rough, so I worked at home. I felt much better for doing so.

When I got back to the office on Tuesday, nobody believed I felt rough. My boss said: "But you and your brother looked fine in the picture."

Andrew

I thought it would be closer. I was wrong. I picked up speed at mile 20 as I thought we'd entered a sprint section. In previous years this section was just a mile long. This time it was 10 miles. I thought Iain was with me and we'd have a race towards the finish but, as the miles passed and I realised that I'd miscalculated, I also realised Iain had not kept up. I was on my own.

I was feeling good. Despite a cold during the week, I was breathing okay and not coughing too much. I kept going, setting small goals for myself. Keep up with this group. Join this chain. Pass these people on Schiehallion. Use the drops on the way to Taymouth.

I know the course so well. We would go on a summer holiday to Aberfeldy, and I've cycled parts of the route many times. It makes such a difference to know the course. You know when to push when to relax and how long it takes between places.

With every mile, I still felt fresh, so I just kept going. I had some gels in my pocket, so I didn't need to stop, so I wondered how fast I could go. I'd hoped to finish in under 4hrs 30 mins. In the end, I finished in 4 hours 11 minutes, the twinner again. That's twin + winner equals twinner (trademark pending)

Iain

"Bum cream?"

I'm standing in a bike shop in Pitlochry, waiting for Andrew to buy an energy gel. Then, I notice a man standing next to me.

"Bum Cream?" He asks again.

I think the man is a shop assistant. I'm not 100% sure – but I hope so.

"Not today, thanks," is the only thing I can think to say.

"Are you sure?"

I wonder why he thinks I need bum cream. Is there a sale on? Does he get commission? Or is there something about the way I walk which made him think – that man needs bum cream.

After leaving the shop, I tell Andrew what happened. He replies.

"It could have been worse. He could have said arse lube".

This year I thought I'd be the Top Todd. Of course, I wasn't, but I did manage to get around without needing bum cream.

Andrew

I won again. Need I say more?

Iain

Let's skip to the Bealach Beag race instead. It was cold and wet during my previous two attempts at Bealach Na Ba. The forecast for this year's race day was also cold and wet.

I packed my winter gear. I wasn't going to suffer because of the weather.

The weather forecast was very wrong. It was the hottest day of the year, and I was dressed like I was about to climb Everest. I should have packed some light kit.

This time I had a road bike. I was well trained and confident of victory. This was going to be my year.

My confidence quickly faded once we reached the climb. There was no wind in the valley of the climb. The temperature must have been near 30 degrees. My very thick woollen top was soaked through with sweat. I was very, very hot.

Andrew sped off. I tried to catch him, but I didn't have the energy. It was like riding in a vertical sauna.

Eventually, I made it to the top. It was a PB for the climb, but I was gutted as Andrew said he had been there for at least 5 minutes. I thought it would have been closer.

It made me even more determined to beat him on the next section.

We had terrific views coming off the hill. The sea looked like it had been imported from the Caribbean. The Isle of Skye was bathed in sunshine. One of those days that made me thankful I am fit and well enough to be out riding my bike.

I then punctured.

I cursed been out riding my bike. Feck. Now I must change the tyre. At least Andrew will help me.

Andrew sped off.

I wasn't alone. A woman came out of a local Bed & Breakfast and asked if she could help. I asked if she could change a tyre. She laughed and said no, but she could fill my water bottle. I changed the tyre whilst she went off with my bottle.

When she came back, she told me how busy her B&B was not at the North Coast 500 passed by. However, all the cyclists who came to her were always exhausted. This is because so many of them underestimate how difficult the section of the road is after Bealach Na Ba.

I thanked her and headed on. I didn't bother racing. Andrew would be finished by now, another year gone, another second place.

Andrew

And again, proving that if you don't succeed at first, then not only must you try, try and try again, you must also be aware that those who do succeed will also try, try and try again too.

Iain

If we're talking proverbs, then I have one for you: "All work and no play makes Jack a dull boy".

Famously, it features in the film The Shining. I thought the phrase was written in Stephen King's novel, on which the film was based, but it was first used in a book by James Howel in 1659. Little is known about James other than, based on the phase, he worked with a man called Jack who was a bit of a workaholic and didn't know how to party like it was 1659.

The phrase is a great one for sport. Some people can be so

obsessed with running/biking or yoga that they have no other interests. I know because I've been Jack.

Andrew

Been?

Iain

When I took part in L'etape du Tour, I became obsessed with the race to the detriment of any other interests. I trained every weekend, and I read everything there was to read about it. I took part in the race, and then I became depressed.

I'd done my life cycling goal, even if I hadn't finished it. I'd trained and started and given it my best shot. So, what next? Do I do it again? Do I do it faster?

I thought maybe a different race was what I needed, so I researched other big races. None of which excited me. I was still depressed. Then I realised it. I wasn't depressed: I was bored with myself. I'd become a one-dimensional person. I was a biker but nothing else. And, if I was bored of myself, Christ knows what anyone else thought of me.

Andrew

No comment.

Iain

I vowed from that moment on always to vary my interests. For every sporting hobby, I would have a non-sporting hobby too. Since then, I've tried stand-up comedy (badly), acting (badly) and painting (badly).

My art tutor taught me how to paint fruit and how to paint people, so he shouldn't have been surprised when my graduation piece ended up being a fruit that looks like a person. Both my wife and Andrew's wife had nightmares after seeing the portrait of what can only be called Lemon Maradona because it looks like a lemon with the startled face of Diego Maradona.

This makes me slightly proud: at least it's not dull.

Andrew

It's not dull, I'll give you that. Its eyes follow you around the room like a human centipede. Its features are best described by the words "Strike me blind." It has a presence in a room like an almighty fart. If Satan had a gallery, Lemon Maradona would be its Mona Lisa.

Iain

I've also painted Andrew. Now, the picture has a presence in a room like an almighty fart.

However, when I wasn't painting, I had a new cycling goal for this year. A planned family vacation in Tenerife inspired me to tackle the highest mountain on the Island: Tiede.

Although my first impressions of Tenerife were slightly strange - in front of me, a large man, with a massive beer belly, was rubbing suntan lotion onto his naked upper body and face. I could barely see his skin due to how thick the white cream was covering him. This is a weird day, I thought. I was sitting on a fake concrete beach in a water park in Tenerife. A giant plastic elephant was staring at me, and five minutes previously, I'd screamed my way down a water slide at 80 km per hour. Quite frankly, the day couldn't get any weirder. It did.

The fat fake albino turned to a young child, who I assumed was his son. The Dad raised both hands and made a grasping motion whilst shouting, "Grrrrrrrrrrr! Grrrrrrrr! Grrrrrrrrrrrrr!"

The Dad then stomps around in a circle. "Son – What am I?"

A mentalist? I thought.

The son stared blankly at the Dad. The Dad opened and closed his hands. He shouted louder, "GRRRR! Grrrrrrr! GrrrrrrRRr! Son – What am I?"

The Dad's big fake white belly, fake white arms and fake white face dripped whiteness all over the floor.

"Dad – I don't know!"

The Dad continued stomping round in a circle. "Grrr! Grrrrrr!" The Dad opened and closed his hands in an animated grasping motion. He asks a final time: "SON! What am I?"

The son was nearly in tears. "Dad! I don't know... I don't know!"

The vast white belly-busting beast stopped stomping around. He lowered his hands.

"For f**ks sake, son. I'm a polar bear. A frigging polar bear!"

The son looked at his Dad. He thought for a second and said, "Polar bears live in the Arctic. It's cold there. The bear wouldn't go grrrrrr it would go brrrrrr!"

I couldn't help admire his logic while at the same time getting on my bike and riding as fast as I could away from this lost polar family.

If you don't know, Tenerife is the largest of the Canary Islands, 200 miles off the west coast of Africa. For years' cyclists such as Bradley Wiggins have come to Tenerife to escape the bad weather at home or, if you're Lance Armstrong (and not Bradley Wiggins (or his lawyers)), also used to escape drug testers.

I wasn't here to train, but I was glad to escape the bad weather as it was snowing at home. I was on a family vacation, but I had one day to cycle by myself.

I decided to attempt the iconic Mount Tiede climb. Tiede is the volcano that dominates the island landscape. The road to it reaches a height of 2250m. It's not the highest road climb in Europe, but it is the longest continuous ascent as it starts from sea level and doesn't flatten out or go down until you get near the top.

I was staying in the southern town of Adeje. I had an all-inclusive deal which meant the most challenging part of the ride was resisting ordering free beers the day before. Initially, I'd planned to climb Tiede via the most direct route, i.e. Adeje to Los Christianos and then TF-28, TF- 51, TF-21, but I'd driven that route previously and got scared by a) the amount of traffic on TF-28 and the steepness of TF-21.

I frantically googled other options and settled on a longer climb which was supposedly on a much quieter road: Adeje to Guia de Isora via TF-82, then up to Aripe to join the TF-38.

I set off as soon as the sun came up. I was slightly apprehensive as cycling on Spanish roads always scares me due to how cars approach and enter roundabouts. The climbing started from the moment I left the hotel. The first section of the TF-82 was tranquil. I barely so a car or person.

The roundabout at the start of TF-82 was scary. Multiple lanes and lots of fast cars. I did what any coward would do in my situation. I got off my bike and used the pedestrian crossings to get around it. Once on the TF-82, the road was quiet to Guia de Isora. The road has a large hard shoulder, so it didn't come near me even when a car did pass at speed.

At this point, I realised I'd made an error and forgot to take any money with me. Instead, I had two bottles of water and seven gels. I decided that would hopefully be enough and, if not, I could always ask another cyclist to lend me a Euro for water.

The following section was challenging. The town of Aripe was so steep I had to push my bike through it. I made the mistake of leaning my bike against a wall to take a picture to demonstrate how steep it was. Unfortunately, the bike fell, and one of my water bottles fell out and rolled back down through the town. I had to walk down and then do the climb again!

Once onto the TF-38, it's a straightforward 23KM climb up onto the volcanic desert of Tiede. The road surface was terrific, and there was hardly a car on it. The road cuts through the forest below Tiede, which helpfully meant a lot of the ride was shaded from the sun.

I climbed 5km at a time before stopping to admire the view and drink some water.

The last section was the desert: great views but busier roads. I cycled until I reached Los Rocques. The last high point before it dips down to the road to the cable cars that take tourists to the top of Tiede. I didn't bother with that bit as I'd been there by car. There isn't much to see other than a toilet and a load of tourists queuing for tickets and the loo.

I went down the direct route to Los Christianos. The road was busy the closer I got to sea level. By the end, it was a little too busy for my liking. I spotted some professionals going up: Team UAE, Team Astana, and Team Chris Froome on the way down. He's a team as he was the only one I passed who didn't have teammates. For some reason, he was training by himself with just a Sky car for the company. Or maybe, it was only the car that could keep up with him.

All the teams were going up the hill faster than I was going down. Which shows you how quick they are and how much of a big Jessie I was when descending.

Andrew

While Iain was trying foreign climbs, I kept to my promise to stay in the UK. I ventured only as far as the border with England by entering The Dirty Reiver 130 (80 miles), a gravel race along the access roads that service the vast areas of forest covering the border of Scotland and England.

A gravel race is an off-road race, and, as such, you don't want to use a road bike. The clue's in the name: Road bike for roads. Off-road bike for going off the road. It should have been obvious but, oh no, not me, I knew better. Or, as it turned out, worse. I knew far, far worse.

The Dirty Reiver started in 2016, and it's based at Keilder Castle in Northumberland, an area of the country that I, and it turned out, the mobile network, have never been.

Keilder is home to Europe's largest artificial lake, though why there's a lake in the middle of Northumberland is not something that's mentioned in any of the leaflets I checked at the castle. It's certainly not there because it's easy to get to because Keilder is in the middle of a large moor crossed by single-track roads, then extensive forests crossed by slow winding B-roads.

It's beautiful, but it's the kind of beauty that demands patience – and an ability to ignore the tractor blocking the way in front of you.

We drove down on Friday and registered on Friday night, though you can register before the race too. We stayed in the town of Bellingham, which was on 30 minutes from the start, though an early start of 5:40 was needed as the race started at 7 am.

Usually, bike races start early to avoid traffic – so I wasn't sure why a race with no traffic needed to start so early. But, I also thought I could use a road bike, and I wasn't any better at predicting timings.

"Maybe six hours?" I said to Iain.

Nowhere close.

Race day had ideal weather. Sunny-ish. Not too warm. A very light breeze and, as it had been dry all week, the trail was dusty rather than muddy.

It was cold to start but nothing that emergency use of a Glasgow Tri Club buff couldn't fix after I realised that I'd forgotten to bring gloves.

Did I tell you how well prepared I was for this race...?

The race started in waves of around 20-25 bikes with a sharp drop from the castle then straight into the forest. The first couple of miles were okayish. A steady climb. A dirt track then…

Ouch!

The first descent.

Crickey!

Another stone.

Blimey!

And another.

Jings!

And another.

And I'd only gone one metre.

One hundred metres of descent later, and I feel like Godzilla has kicked me in the baws, then grabbed my arms, shaken me about, and punched me in the back.

And only another 78 miles to go.

It was horrendous. Every bump, stone, rock and pebble went straight through my bike and into me. I had to pull on my brakes through any descent just to keep some control.

I was going slower downhill than I was going uphill.

It was HORRIBLE.

And I knew then that my estimate of six hours was utterly wrong.

The first hour followed a pattern of grinding up a hill, with slate and pebbles sliding away beneath my wheels, to trying to go down hills as slowly as possible so as not to go over my handlebars or become an involuntary eunuch.

I hated every minute of it.

And, to make things worse, Iain was on a mountain bike and making the whole thing look easy as, every hill, he was picked up by Godzilla and given a soothing massage by Japan's green-skinned spawn of the Nuclear bomb through the magic of suspension and fat tyres.

Not that I didn't have the right tyres. The organisers had recommended 33-inch tyres as a minimum, and that's what I had. But I needed more than the minimum, and I needed big knobbly tyres and shock absorbers. Instead, I got BATTERED.

The route itself was spectacular, with the scenery changing every 10 miles as you go through forest, moors, farmland, dirt track, walking trails and, thankfully, blessedly, a five-mile stretch of smooth, smooth tarmac.

There's even a river crossing.

But it was tough and my lack of a 'granny gear' meant every hill was a challenge, and my lack of springs in my bum meant I'd never sit down again.

After eight hours, we finally got back to Keilder castle. I had to: stop once to reattach my back wheel after all the shaking had separated it loose from the frame and stop twice to stop my nose bleeding after all the shaking separated it loose from my brain. And stop umpteen times to stop shaking.

I'm glad I took part. I now know what it's like to race a gravel race and to race off-road, but I don't think I'll be signing up for another anytime soon. Not without a mountain bike – and not without a doctor's note that I can still father children. However, the most important thing was that we crossed the line together. Despite his support, my victories were still complete as we approached another Caledonian Etape, which this year featured a crucial change as the route was going to increase with the addition of another hill loop.

Runners love change because change represents variety.

I usually try and run different routes each time I go out so that while I might follow streets or paths I've run before, I try and not have too much of a fixed route in my mind. That way, I can change direction, pick a side road I've not in a while or, my new favourite hobby, run along a back alley and find the secret routes through Glasgow hidden behind houses, offices and shops. Running's all about the route, not the destination.

Cyclists, on the other hand, hate change. When you're on a bike, while it's nice to explore new routes, it's also reassuring (and safe) to ride the roads you know well. The ones where traffic is light, where you're not likely to meet an unexpected pothole, and you can concentrate more on the destination than the route. You have somewhere to get to, and you want to get there in the fastest possible time.

That's why I was disappointed to find out that the Etape Caledonia had a new route. Not much of a change, an extra three miles to incorporate a short climb before Loch Rannoch, but a change, nonetheless.

After several years of getting faster and aiming to beat four hours, an extra three miles means that history is lost. I can't compare this year with previous years as we're now riding a new route.

And while the new route will be good – any ride in Perthshire is good – it's also bad as it means the history is lost.

But would it also mean that I would lose too?

Iain

Andrew and I were nearing the end of the race when I began to increase my speed. Just a little. Just enough to see if he'd keep up. I went a little bit faster, and I started building a gap when I heard him shout.

"IT'S NOT A RACE!"

I knew then that I'd won.

The weather forecast was for sunshine. It hadn't rained in the week before the race. Unsurprisingly, it was wet at the start.

We were off at 0632, which meant we got away before most riders. The first five miles were uneventful until we came to a corner. I could see the road kicked up after the corner, so I changed to a lower gear before I got there.

As I took the turn, I heard the unmistakable sound of a gear clanking away and coming loose as some poor rider tried to get into a lower gear. I thought to myself, "What idiot wouldn't notice the hill! You'd have to be a right twat not to change gears in advance. Who'd be that stupid?"

"IAIN!!!" I heard Andrew shout, I looked around: the idiot was Andrew.

Impressively he'd managed to wrap his chain around his bike crank in such a way it was impossible to pull off. Thankfully a moto-bike mechanic turned up. He looked at it and said, "Wow! I've never seen one wrapped that tight." Thankfully after ten minutes of pulling and chain splitting, we were able to sort it.

I could at any point have cycled off to ensure I'd win the race. I stayed. Not because I'm nice, but so I could spend the rest of the ride reminding Andrew that I could have ridden off and, therefore, he should declare me champion by default.

We finished together, but Andrew knows in his heart I won.

Andrew

I know in my heart it was a draw. I'll give him that. I'm not giving him the victory. He had to beat me fair and square. The pressure was on. Like Queen Elizabeth's hairdresser, he was in touching distance of the crown.

Iain

The following January 2019, I read eleven books. During February, I read zero. Nothing. Nowt. Not even a single word. What was the difference between January and February? In January, I was on my honeymoon, and I had hardly any access to the internet or television. During February, I had unfettered access to the internet and television. I checked my internet usage using my iPhone's screen time app. It showed that I was on my phone for 18 hours a week. That is time I could be reading a book... probably two books.

So, I instigated #ScreenFreeSaturday and #SlightlyLessScreenTimeSundayToFriday. (I need to work on the slogan for the second one.)

The rules were simple. On a Saturday:

• No TV

• A phone is allowed but not for web browsing or social media.

• WhatsApp and Facebook Messenger are allowed

On the rest of the week during the hours, 8 pm to 7 am

• TV is allowed

• A phone is allowed but not for web browsing or social media.

• WhatsApp and Facebook Messenger are allowed.

It could be argued that WhatsApp and Messenger should be blocked too, but I class them as communication tools in the same way as a phone call or a text message should be allowed. Blocking communication from friends and family is not the point of the exercise. It's stopping mindless consumption of information, i.e. status updates, tweets etc.

Within a week of starting it, I finished a book. I watched TV and concentrated on the show instead of having one eye on the TV and one eye on Twitter. I also had to face the truth – sometimes it's good to have screen-time.

In that regard, I caved in on #ScreenFreeSaturday and used a screen. I wanted to watch the telly in the evening. I'd done a race; it was a long day of driving, and I just wanted to switch my brain off. Saturday is a day I usually watch a film or something on the telly in the evening, so it was hard to go cold turkey. Instead, I did #ScreenFreeSunday, which was still hard, but I managed it. And while #screenfreesturday was a DNF, I dealt with it correctly. I changed my plan so that I could succeed in future. An approach I followed for this year too.

Having lost every Bealach Na Ba race, I decided to change my plan for this year's race. I decided to take radical weight saving action to eke out the best performance from my bike. I removed the bike's bell. And just in case that was not enough, I also had a backup plan. At the start of the race, we were both given a time dibber. We had to dib in at the beginning and dib in at the finish to record our time. At the start line, I let Andrew dib in first. I then deliberately waited for 10s before I dibbed in.

The race was close all the way around. He was slightly faster on the hills, but I was marginally faster on the flatter sections. We came into the straight finishing side by side. We both raced for the line. Andrew just beat me to it. He celebrated his win. I didn't say anything. I knew he hadn't beaten me by 10s so that I would be faster in the official results. I let him boast. It would make my reveal even sweeter.

We both went to collect out times. He asked what I got. I told him. He demanded to check it. He demanded a second opinion. He wanted the organisers to review the dibbers to see that it hadn't registered incorrectly. I told him how I'd won. He was gutted but did I beat him?

If you look at our times on Strava, it clearly shows Andrew beat me by five minutes. He did the Bealach climb five minutes faster than me. He paused his Strava at the top until I appeared. He then restarted it, and we continued the course.

Is the winner of a race the person who crosses the finish line first, the one with the fastest Strava time or the person with the fastest time? All I'll say is that on paper, I am the fastest Todd of Bealach Beag.

I'd done it.

Andrew

He hadn't.

Iain

I was the fastest.

Andrew

He wasn't, and the Etape proved that again.

Before driving up the start, I was walking along a neighbouring street, and an older man ran out the front door with a woman shouting after him. As he got in his car, she screamed at him: "I don't know why I stay with you!" before she slammed the front door shut and he drove off.

The next day there was a 'For Sale sign on their house. I tell this story because it had two bright points despite the sadness of an imploding relationship. One, I always liked their home, so I finally got to see inside it when the estate agent posted photos on Rightmove. Two, it just goes to show that you need to follow through with actions to back up your words. There's no point shouting about something unless you do something about it, just like the Etape.

Every year I say I'll beat Iain, and every year I beat Iain. I do not count 2018 as a win for Iain despite what he claims. To be fair, he did wait while I had a mechanical, so he could have won if he'd carried on. But he didn't, so he didn't. Nice guys do indeed finish last.

This year I looked at him, and I could see 'runners up place' in his eyes. He had a haunted look on the start line. He looked old, weighed down by a history of failure. The result was a foregone conclusion. It was only a matter of turning up and collecting my winner's medal and goody bag, which should be a baddy bag as there were never any goods in the bag. The bag is always empty. Don't expect a banana or a biscuit or anything at all at the Etape. One year, all it had in place of a treat was a single page flyer for a new Sainsbury's… that was opening later that year. And, in fact, it never opened at all after local protests. But while I always complain about the bag, Iain never does because he's used to coming home from the Etape empty-handed. But he does have persistence and an understanding that DNF can also mean Not First, and that doesn't matter. Only one person can be first (me), but that doesn't mean that everything else doesn't matter. You don't need to know what you're doing, and you don't need to finish. DNF means turning up.

Transition Two: Yoga

Iain

What do yoga instructors have for breakfast?

Ommmmmmmmmmmmmmm....lette!

"Om" is a mystical, spiritual sound often heard in yoga classes. Another sound often heard in class is a fart, but this is neither mystical or spiritual. If it was then eating beans would be a much more enlightening experience.

I try to go to a yoga class once a week. I often fail. It is claimed that Yoga is a journey. In my case, it's a journey with many stops, detours and wrong turns.

During a class I tend not to pay too much attention to the spiritual side of the practice because I've got enough on my mind trying to work out where my arms and legs should be.

But I do pay attention to one statement: the teacher mentioned that one of the aims of yoga is to have an absence of rgo.

That's a great goal!

Just one minor point – if yoga is the absence of ego, why is the yoga studio named after them, and why is their name in massive letters above the door?

Andrew

I like the idea of yoga more than I like yoga itself. I've tried going to yoga classes and what I found was that while I can feel the benefit of stretching and contorting and balancing on one toe, I hate all the omming and ahmnning and "show your body you love it" nonsense that most yoga teachers spout. The one time I tried to show my body I loved it, I was thrown out.

I went to one class in Glasgow city centre that would play whale noises for an hour while the teacher would talk about the mystical link between nature and movement. Whenever she spoke about how we walked taller when the sun came out,

I couldn't help thinking that there is nothing mystical about it: it's Scotland; we're only walking taller because we're not doubled over by the driving rain and wind.

The same class would always end with five minutes of relaxation. This involved lying on your back while the teacher urged you to close your eyes, sink into the mat and appreciate the benefit of the corpse pose. I didn't go back. One hour of whale noises and corpses was not my idea of a fun night out. For the same reason, I'll never watch Blackfish.

I've tried other classes. I used to go along to a Saturday morning class run by a very tall man who could make himself very small just by curling up. He was brilliant. He used to say, "Listen to the sound of your heart, or, if that's not your thing, the air conditioning unit." Mysticism with a choice of reality. That was more like it. Sadly, the class was cancelled after the air conditioning packed in – we weren't listening closely enough – and I stopped going.

Now that we're in lockdown, I thought it would be good to try yoga again. My wife was trying an online class where people would video conference into the yoga teacher, but my aversion to (a) paying for anything and (b) dialling into a strangers house while we all get near-naked meant I looked at Youtube instead. Surely, Youtube would have yoga videos?

And yes, yes it does. There is yoga for everyone. Including yoga videos which, had I dialled into someone else's cam in a similar state of dress, or undress would have led to a divorce.

But after a few searches for yoga for cyclists, having assumed that would be less mystical and more practical, I found 'Yoga for Adriene'. A woman who seemed just as happy pointing out the air conditioning as my previous Saturday teacher.

And while I'd like to think I'd stumbled on some unknown Youtube teacher after I'd checked out a few more videos, I discovered she's one of the biggest 'stars' of Youtube. My search for a yoga teacher had found Robbie Williams when I thought I'd found a star in the pub.

Oh well, here's a plug for her anyway. And if you fancy that and want to listen to a great song, then Robbie Williams has a song called Angels that no one else has heard.

Iain

A wise man once said: "You should try anything once."

What a stupid saying! There are loads of things I shouldn't try – not even once.

Should I poke a sleeping lion in the stomach? No, I've been mauled by my cat for giving him a friendly tummy rub. Imagine what the king of the jungle would do if I poked him in the guts and called him a fatty fatty bum bum.

Should I paint my body blue, stick on a white beard and demand everyone call me Papa Smurf? No – I'd look like a fat extra from Avatar.

Should I attempt one of the hardest extreme triathlons on the planet? DOH! I entered Norseman.

So, when allowed to do Mysore yoga, I asked will it kill me or open me to ridicule? Thankfully, the answers were "no" and "maybe." I was worried about the maybe,

In a standard yoga class, a teacher leads the students through a sequence of moves. In Mysore, a student leads themselves through a sequence at their own pace. Everyone in the class follows the same sequence, but the pace may be different.

The class starts at 6:30 am, but I could join anytime up 7 am. I need as much beauty sleep as I can get. I turned up at 6:59 am. This meant everyone else had already started.

The Mysore sequence is like building IKEA furniture. If you don't do it in the right order, a bit won't fit where you want, no matter how far you bend it.

Now imagine building a Kevlar wardrobe but only having the picture of a wardrobe as your guide. That's Mysore.

I knew I needed to start by standing at the top of the mat. I also knew I had to finish by lying flat, but I couldn't remember the steps in between.

I looked around the class. One woman was bent over in a position her chiropractor would call "a broken spine". Another girl was wrapped so tightly together only a can opener was going to get her unwrapped.

I decided to do neither of those moves. I attempted a bend from the hip. No one laughed, so I thought I might be onto something. I do a few more bends to waste a few minutes. The teacher comes over "what are you doing?"

"Warming up?"

She says, "Let me give you a guide".

Great! That'll help. She would hand me some pics of people in positions that would be called pornographic if there were a partner involved. She says, "Just do two of these and then three of these."

I look at the diagram. It might as well be in Hindi, as I don't understand any of it. It turns out it is in Hindi.

I do a few more hip bends. I think I might be the best hip bender in the class. I think I might be the biggest bender here. Ummm that doesn't sound right.

She comes back over. "What are you doing?"

"Still warming up?" I reply.

"No, you're supposed to be doing this sequence." She demonstrates it.

"Ahhh, it's that sequence. I understand now." I don't.

She leaves. I bend my hips some more. I think if there were a hip bending competition in the Olympics, I'd win a gold medal unless there was a Russian hip bender. He'd probably cheat, and I'd get silver. I'd be gutted when I hear the Russian national anthem as we stand on the medal podium. Then, years later, it would be discovered he was cheating! He'd get disqualified. I'd be the belated champion, but it wouldn't be the same. Instead of a podium, I'd get my medal through the post. Damn you, Sergei!

She interrupts my daydream, "what are you doing?"

"I've warmed up!" I confidently state.

She takes pity on me. "Just lie down. Do you want a blanket to keep warm?"

"No thanks, I don't like blankets of any size, shape or texture. You might say I have a blanket ban!"

She doesn't laugh. It's probably too early in the morning for chuckles.

I give it five minutes, and when she's busy adjusting/torturing another Mysore student, I sneak out.

The wise man was correct to say, "do anything once", but he should also have said, "Don't do it twice".

Andrew

I must be a wise man. I didn't go back a second time.

Iain

I did. And I doubled down. On vacation, I tried aerial yoga. Which is also known as trapeze yoga, flying yoga or "OMG, I'm going to die yoga".

It's a modern style of yoga that incorporates a low-hanging soft fabric hammock and a mat. Moves are made on a combination of mat and hammock or just hammock.

There was only four of us in the class. My wife, who is a yoga teacher, a German girl who is a yoga teacher and the yoga teacher. I'm not a yoga teacher. I'm not even a particularly good yoga student. I realised I was more out of my depth than a dolphin summiting Mount Everest.

The teacher asked me to test the aerial hammock by sitting in it and then spinning around 360 degrees in the air so he could see if my head touched the ground as I turned past the floor. This didn't seem the most safety-conscious method of testing a hammock. It's like testing a gun by pointing it at my head and asking if I see a bullet comes out when the trigger is pulled.

I spin 360 degrees in the hammock. My head flew past the mat. My hair nearly touched the mat. The teacher said, "you need a higher hammock!"

He adjusted the height higher to remove the risk of decapitation but kept it low enough that there was still a chance of severe head trauma.

We started with some sun salutations. Then, some moves were made with the hammock, i.e. leaning on it or putting a leg up. This meant the activities were more demanding and more intense than a typical sun salutation.

"Good. Now you are warmed up; we can start the class." The teacher said.

I thought that was the start! I looked at the clock to see how long I had to wait until I could escape my aerial deathtrap. Those salutations better count towards my time.

"We will do some inversions. Sit in the hammock. Put your hands like this." He demonstrated a way to wrap his hands around the hammock. I copied him.

"Now spin round. Don't worry; you won't fall out."

I wasn't worried about falling out. I was too busy concentrating on my hands but, now that he's mentioned falling out, that was all I can think about!

I tried to spin. I failed miserably. I can't get my legs over my head. The instructor came over. He watched as I feebly tried to do it again. When I failed, he grabbed my legs and before I could say "NO! I DON'T WANT TO DIE", he's spun me 360 degrees!

"Excellent," he looks pleased. "Now do it by yourself."

He went to help someone else. I tried to spin. I failed. So instead, I stomped my foot loudly on the ground. He assumed the noise came from me stopping after doing a spin. "Did you succeed?"

I looked him straight in the eye and told him the truth. "Yes – all the way around. I did it twice just to make sure."

"Great. Do it again so I can see."

"Umm. I'm tired now…. ummm… I'll show you next time."

The others stare at me, knowing that I cheated.

The teacher heads back to the front of the class. "Let's do some High-Intensity Interval Training…."

"Let's not," I think.

He demonstrated an upside-down hanging in the air stomach crunch.

"Do it 20 times!!!"

I successfully crunch zero times.

Whilst hanging upside down trying to crunch, I noticed a man staring into the studio. I imagine he's saying.

"Is it a bird? Is it a plane? No – it's Superman… sorry. No. On second glance, it's not Superman; it's Iain. It looks like he's hanging from the ceiling in a hammock. He doesn't look well. His face has turned a funny colour of red."

At the end of the class, the teacher asked, "how are you all doing for time?" He didn't wait for an answer. "Great. Let's continue!"

Noooooooooooooooooooooo!

After another ten minutes of "flying," we get to leave. As I heard my partner ask if my stomach muscles hurt after doing the HIIT crunches, I say "No – they feel fine!"

They did feel fine....until the next day when I felt like I'd been used as a punchbag by Tyson Fury.

CHAPTER SIX: RUNNING: 10KS AND HALF MARATHONS

Iain

I always remember the day a yoghurt landed on my head.

It was November 1995. I was jogging along a street in Edinburgh. I'd only recently taken up running as a hobby.

I was listening to my Sony mini-disc player. Which was state of the art technology back then. There were no iPhones or even mobile phones available to me.

If I had to make a phone call, I'd need 10 pence and a telephone box.

Now I carry a phone larger than my mini-disc player and my 10p piece combined, and we call this progress! But, before I could question the benefits of technological evolution and even before I could say: "Is that a Muller yoghurt falling from the sky?" a Muller yoghurt had fallen from the sky. It landed on me, leaving a trail of goo across my forehead.

I looked upwards: a man was laughing from a third-floor window. He was holding a spoon. It did not require Poirot to work out that he was the prime suspect. As much as I was shocked to have been 'Muller'd', I was impressed with his aim. I'm sure I would miss it if I tried to throw a non-aerodynamic yoghurt pot at someone from a height of 30 foot. Thankfully, this incident did not put me off running, although it did put me off Muller yoghurt.

It would not be the first or the last time I've been stuck whilst running. One Christmas in the east end of Glasgow, I passed a group of youngsters. My Spidey sense kicked in: I instinctively knew they were going to pelt me with snowballs as soon as I was far enough away to hit - but not close enough to run after them.

As I passed them, I counted to three and braced myself for the inevitable pelting. One. Two. Three. I got pelted. The gang didn't even wish me a merry Christmas.

Sometimes it is not physical objects that I have to evade, but verbal ones. For example, I was jogging past two schoolgirls eating chips when one of them shouted, "OH MY GOD! I'm going to marry you!". Which was an excellent offer, but I don't think she was serious. She didn't even go down on one knee, as she was too busy eating a chip.

Yoghurt is not the most unusual thing to be thrown at me. That honour goes to a fish supper. It was thrown at me while I was jogging in the Meadows area of Edinburgh. I stopped at a traffic junction and then waited to cross the road. As a car passed me, a fish supper was thrown out of the passenger side window. Battered? Yes, it hit me in the stomach, but I think it was fried if you ask about the fish. A passenger shouted "Ha! Ha!" and the car drove off.

Is it a crime to throw a fish and chip supper at a stranger? Yes – probably. But I would argue the biggest crime is to throw a fish supper away without eating all the chips. This was in Scotland. You don't throw away chips in Scotland; you propose with them.

Andrew

Running 20 years ago was viewed the same way a salad is viewed in Glasgow. You know that some people like it, you know it's healthy, but you can't help but look at it suspiciously and poke it if it comes close. That's the sole reason I can think of why people would either throw things or shout "Run, Forrest, run!" from the film Forrest Gump in the hope you'd keep running away from them.

Iain

They didn't shout "Run, Forrest, run" because you're running. Instead, they called it because you looked simple.

Andrew

I've never had food thrown at me, but I have had water balloons chucked at my back and, once, when running through London, a man pointed a pistol at me from the balcony of his flat. I don't know if it was a real gun, but I do know that I broke finally broke the 100-metre record for real when I saw it.

Today, everyone is running. It's normal. If you throw something at a stranger, then that's assault, not banter. Instead, jogging has become routine. It's no longer a niche hobby or target practice; it's something that anyone can do. This is brilliant because as more people take to the streets, the more I am reminded that a trade unionist in the Clyde shipyards once said that he had a Wimbledon champion among his men even though none of them had ever lifted a racquet.

Now, until Andy Murray becomes a welder on a new Royal Navy frigate, that trade unionist wasn't talking literally. He didn't have Roger Feder screwing rivets. Instead, he was talking about potential. The trade unionist wanted to show that everyone could do something, and perhaps even be the best in the world, if only they had the opportunity to do it.

In April 2020, we had an opportunity to put that theory to the test. We were in the middle of the Coronavirus lockdown, and you couldn't go outside (except responsibly and for essential travel only) without finding yourself surrounded by people running.

With many people working from home or furloughed and unable to work, you could only leave your house to exercise and buy essential items. People were taking the opportunity of being locked up to kickstart new hobbies, including digging out old trainers and heading outdoors for a run.

Six months earlier, even six weeks earlier, the only time you heard about other people running was when Bob from Accounts tried to badger you for sponsorship money to run the London marathon. But, with everyone outside, I couldn't help thinking that now was our chance to see if Pete the Postie is the world's most incredible steeple jumper. Or maybe Mary from Margate can run the 100m faster than Usain Bolt can blink? We could have had the best Olympic squad the world has ever seen.

The only downside to all this exercise and potential fulfilled is that we will be faced with so many emails asking for sponsorship from all the newfound runners – from Derek in Marketing's first Marathon and Carol from HR first 10k... Olympic final. That's the power of potential. A potential we all hold - except Iain, who is destined to finish second - like all of us could be world champions if we just had the opportunity. Which we can do because I've got a world record (which I'll cover in the next chapter), and you could have one too if you start. But where do you start?

Iain

I started like most runners with a 10k race.

Today, I don't like people coming along to watch my races, as races are usually dull. It's not fair to ask someone to stand at a race just to see a few seconds of me running past, and it's not fair on me as I don't want to have to look for them as I plod around. I always miss them, and then they complain that I've ignored them. The only time I've taken someone to a race was when I did my first 10Kin 2011. I said to my girlfriend: "You need to support me. It's a big thing for me to run a 10K. Don't you want to come and cheer me on?"

She replied, "No thanks. It's boring". So she must have known my first point too.

Being a good boyfriend, I made her go to the race. I looked out for her as I ran. I was hoping for a shout of "Go, Iain!" Or "Iain, you da bomb!" Which is what the cool kids said in 2011.

Andrew

Instead, she shouted, "Run, Forrest, run," because if it was yelled at me for looking a bit simple, then they call it at him too for being my identical twin.

Iain

No one shouted anything. After 5k, nothing. After 8k, nothing. After 10k, nothing.

I was raging. I collected my medal and then I went to look for her. I found her near the finish eating a cake.

"That was amazing! Races are so much fun!" She said.

"But I didn't see you," I said.

"I know. I was too busy eating the home baking and having massages." The event had supplied massage therapists, and she had used them all before any runners had come back. The home baking was also for the runners.

So, my first lesson when starting to run is to run for yourself, not for anyone else. And don't bring someone to a race and expect them to support you. They might say they will, but instead, they'll dump you for baking and massages, which was apt in this case as, a couple of years later, she left me for a physiotherapist who loved cupcakes.

Andrew

You can't trust your supporters. I was waiting at the end of one race, a triathlon, when a mother turned to her child and said:

"C'mon, let's get ready to cheer Daddy".

The child asked, "Why?"

"Because he's just finished a big race, and it's a massive achievement".

The child looked puzzled. "Is it?" She asked.

After a long pause, the mother said, "Well, he thinks it is!"

I agree with Iain. You need to race for yourself because no one else can run it for you. You might be able to get motivation from others or from raising money for charity, but if you're going to keep running, you need to keep going because you want to keep going. Running is not obligatory unless you're an escaped prisoner, a politician seeking election, or a leaky tap.

Iain

I get motivation from running in different events. I need the challenge of something new to motivate myself to put on trainers and open the front door. That's why every year, I enter races that I've never entered before, and usually the same one I've entered the year before but never quite managed to finish.

Everyone has a race on their sporting CV that they love to enter despite never starting. I've joined the Bucklyvie 10K more times than I've finished it. It should be called the Did Not Start (DNS) 10k. I've entered it four times and started it once.

My first attempt ended when I discovered how long it took to drive to Buchlyvie from my flat in Glasgow. I didn't want to drive, so I didn't bother going. My second attempt ended when it started raining before I'd left the house. I didn't want to get wet, so I didn't bother going. The third time, I lived much closer to Buchlyvie so that I couldn't use distance as an excuse. It wasn't raining so I couldn't use the rain as an excuse. It was snowing, so I used that as an excuse instead.

The phrase "if at first you don't succeed then try, try again" should be "if at first, you don't succeed and it's not raining, snowing or too far away, then try again."

On my fourth attempt, it was neither raining nor snowing. The race started on a football pitch next to a church. From the start, there was a small lane to the main road. There was a huge puddle in the lane which had no way around it.

I'll run through just about anything. I'll run through the pain barrier, and I'll run through atrocious weather, I'll run through the night. There's nothing I won't run through - except a puddle. I'm not getting my trainers dirty or my feet wet for anyone. So, the race started, and almost immediately, it stopped. It turns out most runners don't like puddles. Everyone gingerly tried to tiptoe through the puddle before running again once they reached the main road.

After the race, I got a text from a friend asking if I'd picked up a post-race goodie bag from the hall. D'oh. I'd forgotten to collect it.

Oh well. The good thing about races like this is that I'll just have to do it again. Hopefully, it will take me fewer attempts to do the next one.

Andrew

Getting to the start line is an achievement. But once you're there, once you're lined up and ready to go, then every race needs an official Starter. If you don't have a Starter, then you don't have a race. You have many people in lycra standing politely and looking at each other to see if anyone else will move first. That's not a race; that's a queue.

You need a Starter. Someone fires the pistol, sounds the horn, drops the flag, fires a smoke cannon, and lets off a hundred fireworks. (that has genuinely happened to me at a race. It was terrific.) But more often, the Starter will be the organizer, a local celebrity or politician or prominent club runner associated with the race. However, the Trossachs 10K had a different approach. A chef started it.

"Good luck," he said, dressed in chef's whites and still wearing his apron as he'd just wandered out of his kitchen, which he had because the kitchen was only 20 metres from the start line. We could see into as he'd left the fire door open.

"Why is the chef starting the race?" I asked Iain.

We couldn't figure it out. He didn't mention a running club, so we assume he wasn't one of the organizers, he didn't mention a charity, so he wasn't one of the beneficiaries, and he didn't plug his restaurant, so he wasn't even looking for publicity.

We can only assume that there was a misunderstanding. Someone must have said they needed a Starter, and someone else thought they'd best get a chef because, if there's one thing chefs know, then it's starters. But we never found out. We just knew it was apt that a chef started the race as the only reason we were racing the Trossachs 10K was that there was a cracking butcher in town, and we fancied a run then pies from the butchers. Sometimes, races are not chosen by your mind but by your stomach.

Iain

The quality of food at the end of a race is one of my main criteria for choosing to do an event, which is why the Balfron 10K is one of my favourites. They always have excellent home baking.

The name Balfron means "village of mourning" in Gaelic. This originates from a legend that the village was attacked by wolves, who stole children out of the villager's homes. To me, this sounds like a story made up by people who'd got rid of their kids and had to think of an excuse when the police investigated.

Policeman: I've heard children have gone missing. Do you know anything about that?

Villager: Not me, officer. I'm innocent. It was those wolves.

Pesky creatures, always wolf-ing around.

Policeman: Wolves, you say?

Villager: Oh yes. [Turns away from the policeman, makes a howling sound] Did you hear that? That was one. He's probably coming right now to steal our kids.

Policeman: You're nicked.

I didn't spot or hear any wolves on the course.

The Balfron 10k is undulating, which is Gaelic for "hilly as f**k". It's an out and back course. And excuse my mansplaining, but I'm going to state the obvious – an 'out and back' approach means you go out and then come back on the same course. I assume all runners understand that, but I had to explain it as one man didn't.

The first half of the Balfron 10k is an undulating farm road. When I wasn't running up a hill, I was running down a hill. The second half of the race is on the same road as the out section.

I got to the turnaround point and mentally prepared myself to run up and down the hills again. The man behind hadn't prepared himself. He turned around and said: "Who put that hill there?"

How could he forget? He was just on it. Have you got the memory capacity of a goldfish?

He screamed "Aaaarghh!" and fell into step, running just behind me.

We came to another hill. I know because he said: "Why is there another hill there?"

Because we ran it on the way out.

He screamed "Aaargh!" again. and continued running just behind me.

We came to the last hill. I know because he said "F**koff hill!" and then screamed, "come on!"

At this point, he ran past me. I noticed he ha was wearing headphones. His music was loud. Why was he talking to himself whilst simultaneously blocking all noise? Is it rude to wear headphones when you are talking to yourself? Does he turn to himself and say, "You're not even listening? You're too busy listening to music!". And maybe he was just frustrated because he had told himself about the hills and now realized that he hadn't heard a word he'd said.

Andrew

I remember that race. I was knackered. I'd bike the day before in Wanlockhead – the highest village in Scotland. It was a 40-mile cycle down through the Mock pass and back via Drumlanrig Castle and Elvenfoot before climbing to the top of a local hill.

Before I started, I parked in the centre of Wanlockhead. A smiling man with a large old rucksack approached.

"Are you here to open the shop?"

I explained I was cycling.

"Oh, my bus leaves in 10 minutes, and I need to buy my licence."

"You need a licence for the bus?"

"No, I need a licence from the landowner as I'm here to find GOLD!"

Which was not what I expected to hear at 9 am on a Saturday when I'm not in California, and it's not the nineteenth century.

"How do you find gold?"

He opened his rucksack and then showed me a tube to collect gravel from the bottom of riverbeds. Next, he showed me a large plastic tray with grooves where the lighter soil would be washed away, but the heavier gold would be caught in the tracks. Then he showed me his pan where he gently washed the last of the gravel, leaving behind the millions and millions of pounds of GOLD!

"Do you find much?"

"I usually find a few specks the size of a grain of salt."

Really?!? I looked round to see his Rolls Royce.

"And how much is that worth?"

"Nothing, not even a pound, but it's FUN!"

I didn't want to hear about fun. I wanted to hear about making millions just washing gravel. But despite, as I found out later, Wanlockhead being known as 'God's Treasure House in Scotland' due to the abundance of minerals found in the area, there's not a lot of gold in "them thar hills".

The licence was £5 (I checked), and if it was possible to make more money panning for gold than selling rights for £5, then you can bet the landowner wouldn't be selling licences for £5.

Despite the slight chance of striking riches, as I cycled around, I began to see that all the people I'd previously thought were fishing was panning for gold instead. It seems that gold fever is alive and well and can be found in Wanlockhead.

Cycling the day before a race did not help my running. I plodded around the course very slowly.

Iain

Andrew fails to mention that the gold miners so inspired him that he bought me a gold mining course as a Christmas present. He also bought a book about gold mining which he planned to give me on Christmas day.

But, when I opened the present, it wasn't a gold mining book. It was a book called 'The History of Elgin'. Andrew looked shocked and then said, "F**K!!!". He'd bought that book as a Secret Santa present for a colleague who was moving to Elgin. It should not have been under our Xmas tree. I should not have opened it: it was meant to be a thoughtful gift to a colleague. Instead, one of Andrew's colleagues was opening his anonymous present and wondering why on earth a colleague had sent him a book called "So you want to be a gold digger?".

Andrew

Some people jump from a 10k to a marathon, like baking a cake and then jumping straight into the Great British Bake Off final. It's possible, but you really might want to try something easier first.

Most folk know the story of why a marathon is 26.2 miles. In 1908, the organizers of the London Olympics had planned a 26-mile race, but, at the last minute, Queen Alexandra asked them to move the start to the gardens of Windsor Castle so the royals could see the race begin and they could finish right in front of the royal box. That added an extra point two to the race.

Not that 26 miles was the proper distance. The Marathon was first to run in the 1896 Olympic Games in Greece in honour of the myth of Pheidippides. He ran from Marathon to Athens to deliver the good news of an improbable Greek victory over the Persian army.

Pheidippides ran the entire 25 miles from Marathon to Athens. Then, after he announced 'Victory!' to the awaiting Greeks, he collapsed from exhaustion and died probably because he forgot to wear clothes. Or trainers.

So, the 1896 race became the marathon in honour of the town, and the distance was set at 25 miles to replicate his achievement. Before it became 26 miles – presumably because no one died the next time they ran it, and they wanted to keep making it longer until someone did. Sadists. Thank the lord for Queen Alexandra putting a stop to it all.

(This explanation may not be true, but, as I can't find any other reason, it's as good as any.)

In Scotland, you don't need to go straight to a marathon as one of my favourite 10k races isn't 10k at all. Instead, it's the Kirkintilloch 12.5k, which presumably has an equally inspiring story of why they've added an extra point two five to the race. Except... I can't find one. So, I'm just going to make it up.

The Kirkintilloch 12k used to be 10k after Shug McGlinty ran between Cumbernauld and Kirkintilloch to celebrate Clyde FC finally winning a match against East Stirling. Just like Pheidippides, he was stark naked and, just like him again, he died when he reached the end because, well, Scotland in February. I don't go out without at least a scarf, gloves, woolly jumper, bobble hat and a three-bar heater.

The original route was 10k, but Queen Elizabeth lived in a semi-detached beside the finish line, and she wanted to see the winner while she prepared toast for Prince Philip in the morning.

Hence, the Kirkintilloch 10k became the Kirkintilloch 12.5k, and we have a unique race on the Scottish running scene.

Or, if you don't believe that story, here's another one: just try running it. The Kirkintilloch 12k has 12 hills in 12 kilometres, which is 11 too many. However, it is well named, with its extra point two five, because it does make you feel like you've run a marathon and, just like Pheidippides, you'll want to keel over at the end.

Iain

I love it too because I finally managed to work out the answer to the question, "when you run, do you stare at other runners' bums?"

It's hard not to stare at arses unless you have a perfect upright running style. I run slightly stooped forward in a way that naturally brings my gaze to tush level.

I thought about this when I saw a photo of myself and a man in a white t-shirt from the Kirkintilloch 12.5K. I didn't know who the man was, but I ran with him for about 15 minutes. I hadn't seen his face until I saw the photo. He was slightly quicker than me, so I spent all that time just a couple of meters behind him in a perfect eye to the posterior running position.

I was with him for a quarter of the race, but if I were asked to pick him out of a police line-up, then I'd have to ask him to turn around. It's only his bahookie that I'd recognize. I suspect my butt to face ratio in a race is at least nine butts for everyone face I see.

Kirkintilloch is the perfect place to discuss derriere's because the town is known as "The Canal capital of Scotland", which is proclaimed on a billboard as you enter the town. But why does that make it an arse friendly town? Well, when you look at the billboard, you will see, if you look closely, people paint over the "C" in canal.

Andrew

When I started running at university, I would, as I've said, run on a treadmill for 20 – 30 minutes on a Monday, Wednesday and Friday. Over a year, it became part of my weekly routine as I was studying for my final exams. Then, one day, my knee hurt.

"That's nothing," I thought. "A wee run will fix that!"

I'd pop up to the university gym and, after five minutes, the pain would start to fade, and, after 20 minutes, it would be gone.

"See," I thought, "it was just a wee niggle!"

And by the time I'd have my shower, my leg would fall off.

Not literally. I'd topple. But it might as well have as I couldn't use it for the rest of the day. It wouldn't bend; I couldn't put weight on it; I would hop from gym to library to home until -

I'd wake up in the morning, my knee would hurt, and I'd think:

"It's nothing; a wee run will fix this!"

And I was a cripple for a month until I realized that a 'wee run' will only fix this if your problem is an escaped lion, and you need to get away fast. If your problem is a damaged ligament, then don't run on it.

You need to follow the RIC (Rest, Ice and Compression) program, not the RIC (Run, Ignore, Crawl to Bed) program.

That's why small steps are better than giant leaps. Don't go from 10k to a marathon; try to run a bit further or a bit faster, and then see how you get on. However, it is vital to learn good technique as, if you don't start on the right foot, then there's nothing a long run will fix that a wee run has already broken.

Iain

The first running race I ever entered was the Glasgow half marathon in 2001. I tried to find my result, but all I found was a paragraph in the then Glasgow Herald: "Congratulations to the 7,625 runners who completed the race. Results will be available in Glasgow libraries from Friday."

Imagine entering a race now in which you only got your result a week later in a library. For any millennials reading this, libraries are Kindles made of bricks. And for any teenagers reading this, blimey, how are you doing that? I didn't even know we were on YouTube.

I love books. When we were young, Andrew and I would go to the local library in the morning to get a book each. We'd read the book in the afternoon and then return to the library to get another book to read in the evening. Yes – we were the cool kids in school.

Anyways, Andrew and I and one of his friends had entered the race. Andrew's friend arrived at the start wearing a backpack that wouldn't have looked out of place on a Sherpa climbing Everest.

"Are you off to climb a Munro?" I joked.

The Sherpa didn't laugh.

"No. I brought the backpack to carry my juice." He pulled out a two-litre bottle of orange.

I stared at it and said: "'You do know you get water on the course? You don't need to bring your own."

He looked at me like I was an idiot. "Of course I know that. That's why I brought diluting juice!" He'd brought a two-litre bottle of Robinson's diluting orange juice.

How much juice can a man drink!? He either gets very thirsty, or he was planning to open an orange juice stall.

The race started.

Someone from the crowd spotted the Sherpa and shouted, "are you running up Mount Everest?". He didn't laugh. Thirty seconds later, a woman from the crowd called, "are you running up Mount Everest?". He still didn't laugh. This was going to be a long day.

While he remained silent, later, I did hear one runner react to a shout from the crowd. I was running alongside an older woman and her daughter. The daughter proudly shouted at her mum, encouraging and praising her, "you can do it, Mum!". It was so sweet to see them share this special moment across the generations. It became even better when the mum took one look at the daughter and thanked her by shouting, "Why don't YOU just F**K off.? I NEVER wanted to do this. I wanted your Gran to live!".

I didn't ask.

My race was uneventful until I got to the nine-mile point. I wanted to beat the other two. I looked at them. They weren't paying attention so I started running as fast as I could. I'd run fast until I got to the finish line.

I ran hard. I saw the 10-mile sign in the distance. Not far to go now. One last push...I ran hard. I looked for the finish line...but there was no finish line. At this point, I realized a half marathon is half a marathon and not, as I mistakenly thought, 10 miles.

I felt a bit stupid, and the fast run had tired me out. I had to walk. The other two caught up with me.

"Why did you run off?" Asked Andrew.

I told them the truth...sort of.

"I was desperate for the loo....ummm...yes...that's why."

They continued running. I walked the last three miles until I got to the finish. I met Andrew and the Sherpa. The Sherpa offered me some juice. I said yes

He opened his bag to get it but pulled out a pair of boxing gloves.

"WTF!!!" Said the expression on my face. "Why did you run with them?"

"This is my boxing bag. Where else would I keep them?"

If nothing else, I had to admire his logic.

At the end of the race, I asked why he ran with his bag and if he would have found it easier to run without it. He then explained that he was a postman and he liked to run while delivering the post. However, he was so used to running with a bag that he now couldn't run without one. Which also made sense and explained why he ran up to people's front doors on the way round.

Andrew

The technique is essential. I don't know anything about technique, but it was the technique that helped me clinch a world record from Iain. I say "world record" but, as world records go, it's very much a 'local' world record as I have a world record in running to the top of the highest point in Stornoway, which is not even the most famous thing in Stornoway, never mind the Isle of Lewis.

Iain

Until recently, the Isle of Lewis was famed for three things: Harris tweed, sheep and rocks. The stone is called Lewisian gneiss, and it's a group of rocks three billion years old. The only rock group older is The Rolling Stones.

However, that changed in 2016. Today, the Isle of Lewis is also famous as the ancestral home of US President Donald Trump. This is why in 2018, instead of starting the Stornoway half marathon with the classic countdown – "3, 2, 1, go!" rather, it went "3, 2, 1… WTF! IS THAT DONALD TRUMP?"

The Donald starting the race wasn't the real Donald. It was a local in a bad wig. Trump's mum came from a small village near Stornoway. A generation later, he made it to Washington and was in charge of the free world. My mum also left a small village near Stornoway, but I've only made it to Glasgow a generation later, and all I'm in charge of is a cat. Note to self: must try harder.

It's a pity it wasn't the real Donald Trump. I'd like to have heard him address the runners in his own inimitable style.

"This year's race is THE greatest running event Stornoway has ever seen. We're going to make a lot of runners happy today. Believe me.

"Crooked Hillary was asked to start the race, but she was too busy. SAD.

"Let's make runners great again… 3, 1, start!!! What do you mean I didn't say 2? I said 2. Anyone who claims I did not say 2 is a liar. Fake news".

I've done the Stornoway half marathon a few times. Usually, hungover.

One time I flew home, and within 30 minutes of landing, I was drinking in a pub. The race was the next day, but before I could say, "I'm not drinking tonight; I have a race in the morning" I was drinking, and it was no longer today but in the wee hours of tomorrow, and I was in a nightclub ordering another pint. It could have been my seventh pint of the evening/early morning. It could be my 8th. It could be my 20th. I lost count like I was running the Glasgow half marathon.

The barman asked, "didn't you say you were running a half marathon tomorrow... sorry, today?"

I replied, "what... Ummm... pint... YAY... music! and then started dancing. I say dancing. I know all the right moves; I just didn't know them necessarily in the right order.

The barman laughed, "I'll see you at the start as I'm doing it too".

I didn't listen. I was too busy singing "Do you remember when we used to sing sha la la la la la la la la la la te da"

I made it to the half marathon the next day, but I was so hungover I could not hold the pen to fill in the entry form. Instead, I signed the form with a drunken "X". I was so desperate to get to the first water stop I ran the first three miles faster than I had ever run before.

It was a beautiful sunny day, and the drink poured out of me like a fire hose, but I finished the race with a personal best time, and I was top in his age category. (I admit that was because I was the only person in my age category). I spent the rest of the day in bed regretting every pint I had consumed and vowing never to drink before a race ever again - but I did the same the following year.

The night before the race, I was back in the nightclub drinking until 3 am. At this point, I should have gone home, but instead, I went to a friend's house to drink some more. I stopped drinking when I realized I had a race to run. I phoned my dad and asked him to collect me and bring my running kit.

I struggled to stand correctly on the start line. The whole world was moving back and forwards, or was that me? I told my dad to wait ten minutes and then drive along the course and check in on me. If I felt terrible, I'd quit, and he could give me a lift back.

The race started: everyone else started running, I followed. I knew all the right steps, just not necessarily in the right order. I fell over. I got up. I lasted five minutes and then threw up. I scanned the road, hoping to spot my dad driving towards me. There was no sign of him; I wanted to stop. I checked my distance — 13 miles to go.

I jogged on. My head hurt, and I was rough as a skunk with a drinking problem, no coordination and a yoghurt pot on its head. I scanned the road again for my dad. No sign of him. 12 miles to go

I restarted my death march. The world was spinning before my eyes, and I wanted to go to bed. Still no sign of him. 11 miles to go.

Nothing. 10 miles to go.

Where is he? Nine miles to go.

Oh, God. I think I'm going to die. Eight miles to go.

What do you mean the next four miles are uphill???? Seven miles to go.

This was harder than climbing Mount Everest in underpants and just a rucksack filled with boxing gloves, orange squash and no water. Six miles to go.

I see him! YES! Screw this race. I'm out of here....oh. That's not him. Just a car that looks similar. Oh, Lord. Make this end. Five miles to go.

If I drink all the water at this water stop, will it dilute the alcohol and make me feel better?

Four miles to go.

Downhill. Weeeeeeeee. I'm flying now. Three miles to go.

I think I'm last. Two miles to go.

I'll kill my dad when I see him. One mile to go,

There's a big crowd at the finish line. They spot me. They start cheering and whooping. The crowd are going wild! One man shouted, "you can do it!" Wow, I didn't expect such a big reaction. I raise my hand to thank them. They must be impressed by my effort. Wait a sec. I cross the finish line, but the man's still shouting. "You can do it". He doesn't need to say that. I've done it.

I turn around; I'm not the only finisher. They weren't cheering me. They were cheering a man behind me. An 80-year-old man.

After the race, I asked my dad why he didn't come. He said he wanted to teach me a lesson. He certainly did – I never relied on him for a lift again.

I have done the race sober. When running, I like listening to music, and I tend to fixate on one lyric of a song. The lyric repeats in my mind as I run. It becomes a mantra. And repeating this mantra becomes a distraction from running and helps me get through tricky sections of a race. Usually climbs or areas where I'm tired and sore.

During the race, I listened to Scottish DJ Calvin Harris and his song 'I Feel So Close to You Right Now. As I got to a hill, I started repeating the chorus in my mind: "I feel so close to you right now... I feel so close to you right now... I feel so..."

Each time I repeated the lyric, I powered further up the hill. I feel so close to you right now... feel so close to you right now... I feel so...

About halfway up the hill, I passed a female runner. She looked at me. I looked at her. She looked horrified. I realized that I hadn't been repeating the mantra in my mind. I'd been saying it out loud.

No wonder she was horrified. She didn't want a big sweaty, heavy breathing man running after her declaring how close he felt. I ran away. Very fast.

My next mile was my fastest as I ran, repeating the mantra, "I feel so embarrassed next to you right now."

Andrew

That's not the only embarrassing thing to happen on a race-course. Have you ever run a half marathon backwards? Or any race backwards? And by backwards, I mean running the route in reverse – not running backwards yourself, looking over your shoulder and trying not to run into an oncoming car.

We have. For some reason, when we arrived at registration at Kinross in Fife, the organizers didn't have my entry for the Loch Leven Half Marathon.

Loch Leven half marathon is one of my favourite races. It has excellent views of the loch and the surrounding hills. It has some nice long descents and only a couple of longer climbs. Every few miles, the view changes, starting in an industrial estate in Kinross, moving through fields, then Loch Leven, moving closer to the hills, climbing through Scotland well before finishing with farms, fields, rolling roads and a final couple of miles along a trackback to Kinross.

I cannot comment on whether my missing entry may have something to do with me getting my entry wrong in the first place and maybe not, you know, kind of, maybe... not entering in the first place. Though I swear, I thought I had entered at the time.

Since we were there and ready to start, we thought we'd run the race anyway. But, because it wouldn't be fair to join a race without an entry, we thought we'd run the route in reverse.

And everything was fine. The first few miles were quiet, the middle miles saw a flood of runners approach us, and the last few miles saw horrendous rain. Rain so bad that we thought it best to take a shortcut, leave the road and cut across a field to take a trail to Kinross.

Only one problem. The trail didn't go to Kinross; it didn't go anywhere. It stopped beside Loch Leven. Which, unless we wanted to swim for it, was not going to be runnable. So, we ran across another field.

A cow got mad.

We ran back. We got lost. We eventually ended up back at the road we'd left. Wet. Tired. No further forward. We ran to the finish/start and checked our mileage – 15 miles, for a 13 mile half Marathon ran in reverse. There's a lesson here about constantly checking your entry before going to the start of a race. Either that or always carry a compass if you want to take a shortcut.

Iain

What was worse than getting lost was that Scottish Athletics had banned headphones during road races. This is a major issue for me because I have to listen to Andrew's chat instead of listening to music.

This was his "banter" from the half marathon. He spots a tree – "Look, there's a tree!". He spots a hill – "Look, there's a hill!". He spots a sheep – "Look, there's a cow!". Animal recognition isn't one of his strong points.

Andrew

I like listening to headphones when I run, usually Podcasts, occasionally music, sometimes the radio.

I can understand that organizers want to keep runners safe. But banning headphones seems over the top. Why not just say those runners with headphones run at their own risk?

This isn't much, given that statistics showed that "SERIOUS ACCIDENTS TRIPLE WHEN WEARING HEADPHONES", as one headline put it. This sounds serious, but it only involves 47 accidents a year in the United States, up from 16 to eight years earlier.

This is not to belittle the 47 accidents which occurred. Merely to point out that half of the accidents involved people struck by a train at railway stations - not somewhere you usually go for a run - and perhaps studies like these are not appropriate when judging people running on roads and trying hard not to be hit, especially if they're running backwards.

Saying that, if I get hit by a car tomorrow while out for a run, please stop reading this book. I don't want to die an ironic death.

Iain

It's hard not to listen to music as we carry our phones with us everywhere. You need to because you still need to be called even when running, like when I was trying to register for the Balloch To Clydebank Half Marathon. Andrew was on the phone with me.

"Where are you?" he asked.

I replied: "I'm in the car park."

I had agreed to meet him at the official race start – Clydebank Leisure Centre. I was parked in the car park, and I thought it was pretty easy to spot as it wasn't too full of cars.

"Where in the car park? I don't see your car."

I looked around. I was the only car in my part of the car park. It was obvious. "I'm the only one here. Look towards the back of the car park."

"I can't see you. There's nobody parked at the back of the car park". He sounded annoyed.

It suddenly dawned on me – "Are you at the old leisure centre rather than the new one?"

"There are two leisure centres???"

"Yes – you've gone to the old one! Idiot"/

Which is why you need your phone. You might need it to phone someone, and you'll need it to find where you're going on Google Maps.

Andrew

In my defence. It wasn't a good start. I was in the back of a taxi and had to point out to the driver that he was driving away from where we needed to go. "Are you sure Clydebank is not back this way?" I pointed. He took one look at the sign saying "Clydebank" behind us and said: "I don't know that way". I asked if he was following his satnav, and he added, "Never use it – it gets things wrong all the time!".

Given I had been tracking him on an app as he approached the house. I could see he'd missed the road, done a U-turn, missed the road again, got caught in a one-way system and had parked for 5 minutes in a layby (I assume to try and work out where he was going), he maybe wasn't one to judge others on directions. Never mind criticizing the location prowess of multiple geo-stationary satellites and the software calculations of Google.

"Can you just turn around, and I'll tell you where to go?"

"We're going the fastest way," he said.

We weren't.

"You won't get there any faster," he claimed.

We would.

"But if you insist…"

I did.

And 10 minutes later, we were in Clydebank for the start of the race and not in Hamilton, which is where we would have gone because that's the way he knew.

On the way over, between giving directions, I could see the weather was turning. Grey clouds were turning black. A few spots of rain became a shower became a power wash from heaven. By the time I left the taxi, I was soaked through just spending 30 seconds looking for Iain.

He wasn't there. Hardly anyone was there.

I phoned him.

"Are you in the car park?"

"Yes!"

"No, you're not. I'm here, and I can't see you."

Then he asked if I was in the right car park as the race start had moved from the old sports centre to the new one.

"Errr…"

I admit it turns out my taxi driver wasn't the only one with no idea of where to go.

Iain

It was an honest mistake to make. The race had always started at the old leisure centre. I drove over to collect him. Several other runners were waiting there. This shows how few people read pre-race instructions as it was pretty clear from the notes where to go.

The race is a point to point from the shores of Loch Lomond back to Clydebank. Clydebank is where the band Wet Wet Wet come from. It was also an apt description of the weather. The rain was hammering it down as I got changed in the car, but thankfully, I had packed a Gore-Tex hat and jacket. Once I had them on, it looked like I was off to climb a mountain rather than run a race.

To get to the start, the organizer put on buses. They must have asked the bus company "How much for a bus to Balloch for 700 runners....HOW MUCH!!! Can you do it cheaper? How much for a bus with no heating?"

The cold, miserable bus ride was more of an endurance test than the race itself. Shortly after leaving Clydebank, the rain turned to snow. The talk on the bus was whether the race would be cancelled. I saw one man in tiny shorts and a sleeveless vest. I don't know what weather forecast he'd seen that morning to be dressed so inappropriately. He must have assumed the yellow weather warning meant "Danger – there may be sunshine".

When we arrived, a man told the bus driver not to leave as he might be needed to take all the runners back to the start. The organizers were consulting and would announce shortly whether the race would go ahead.

We took the opportunity to get into the toilet before anyone else.

When getting on a bus to a race, the critical thing to remember is to make sure you're the first off it. Everyone goes to the toilet when they arrive. The longer you're on the bus, the further behind you'll be in the queue. A queue that gets slower and slower as the toilet roll in the cubicles is used until eventually there's only one cubicle for 200 runners.

Word soon came through that the race would go ahead, but anyone who wanted to go back to the start could get back on the bus. I was happy to run. It had stopped raining, and it didn't feel too cold, although I was worried about ice on the paths.

Runners are a hardy bunch, so most choose to start, including the man from the bus who had hardly any clothes on.

The first couple of miles are along a canal path. After that, there's not much room to pass people, which is annoying as faster runners get caught behind slower ones, which is why I was behind Andrew. Honest.

There was a lot of puddles on the path due to the snow melting. Runners like to think of themselves as hardy souls prepared to run through rain, hail and sleet, but the one thing they won't run through is a puddle. It was amusing to watch the different techniques other runners used to avoid getting their feet wet.

Andrew

The race itself was a challenge to remain warm and comfortable as the weather changed from snow to rain to dry spells to rain again.

Knowing that it might rain, I'd just worn shorts and not leggings. My theory is that leggings don't help in the rain. They get wet, and then your legs get cold as leggings cool you down. You're better off with just your hairy legs – nature's leggings – when it rains.

I don't know if this is true, though, but for half the race, I congratulated myself on my choice as the water dried from my legs during the dry spells. Then, the other half of the race, I cursed my choice as everyone looked like they were running as happy as runners with toasters strapped to their thighs.

Iain

Whether wearing legging or not, sometimes you can't avoid running through a puddle. Some people swerve at the last second to avoid the puddle, and another attempt a long jump to stride over it. After overcoming my initial resistance, I now prefer to go straight through the first puddle I see and let my feet get wet. I then don't have to care about avoiding puddles for the rest of the race. It's a wet race. Just get soaked and then get on with it.

The last few miles of the course usually are run on pavements. The organizers very clearly state, "Stick to the pavements. Do not run on the road." But many chose to ignore this as the pavements were covered in slush. Some were running on the road with headphones on as cars whizzed by. They must not have read the Scottish Athletics' rules, but I'd instead get my feet wet than be hit by a car even with headphones on.

Race organizers should offer an email/text service where you can grass up other competitors to get them disqualified. It would be for people's good as they'd then learn not to do stupid things in races.

Andrew

You can't call the race scenic. There are a few nice spots, mainly at the start as we run along the canal from Balloch, but most of the race is through housing or industrial estates. It does, though, have the advantage of feeling like you're running downhill as there's very few climbs or even gentle inclines, and there are a few long stretches when you run downhill. But at least the finish line is scenic if you like skips and bins.

However, if you don't want to repeat yourself and try and find somewhere more beautiful to race, then here's a tip: turn left.

Last week, I turned left. It wasn't deliberate. It just happened. I'd started running my usual route when someone had locked a gate and blocked access to a short woodland trail five minutes into the run. I had no choice. Instead of turning right, I had to turn left.

In my head, I'm grumbling. All my thoughts of where to run and how far to go had been blocked. How could I run six miles if I couldn't run the first mile? Where would I go?

But, as I ran, a thought took hold. Why not turn left again?

Why not try and run randomly? Whenever I would get to a junction, I would ask myself, "Which road do I know the least?" and that's the way I'd go.

In the process, I discovered a new trial, a new park, and a new interest in running. But I wasn't running; I was exploring.

While there's joy in running the same routes, the comfort of knowing where you're going, what you'll see and the calmness that comes from not thinking about anything at all, there's no spark: the same roads, the same streets, the same pavements, the same beat. No one ever said, "You know what, I find fun, doing the same thing as yesterday and the day before and the year before that".

Last week, I turned left. And while there's fear of getting lost or finding a route that is worse than the one you'd planned, that's a pessimistic view. You might discover crocodiles, mud, or, worse, a long straight road (is there anything more boring than not turning?). You might also find a hill with an escalator. I can but dream.

So, next time you go running, turn left. But remember to turn right at least once. If you don't, you go anywhere. You've just run in a circle.

CHAPTER SEVEN: RUNNING: MARATHON & ULTRA RACES

Iain

I found this quote on Facebook from the Welsh Runner:

"The marathon is such a huge commitment and is a lot of work. But it is the most rewarding race I've ever done. The first time you cross that line is so emotional. The relief, the pain, the tears, it's a moment that will live with you forever."

This quote chimed with me because when I first completed a marathon, I felt… none of those things.

The only thing I felt was my nipples. That sounds weird. Let me explain.

It took me three attempts to complete a marathon. My first attempt was at the Edinburgh Marathon. Andrew had entered the race, and he had trained for months in advance of it. I had not entered or trained at all.

He phoned me the night before the start to say one of his friends had dropped out of the race and did I want the place. I thought about it for a second. I drank some beer. I happened to be a pub at the time he called. "Sure – count me in. I'll see you at the start tomorrow." He hung up. I turned to my friends in the bar. "Sorry guys, but I have to go home. I'm doing a marathon in the morning".

My friends gave me their full support by buying me another beer, "You might as well have one for the road."

Five beers and many vodka shots later, I stumbled out of a nightclub at 3 am. I decided to walk home rather than get a taxi. I knew I had to warm up my legs before doing a marathon.

I met Andrew at the start line. I didn't know the route. If I did, I wouldn't have started. This was the old Edinburgh marathon route. These days it's a relatively flat course, but this one started at Meadowbank Stadium and immediately ran up the side of Arthur's Seat, the dormant volcano that looms over Edinburgh.

I felt rough, but Andrew was chipper. He had got a good night's sleep and had not drunk alcohol in weeks. I was sweating booze. If you licked me, you'd get drunk.

I managed to run until mile 13; then, I spotted a bus heading to Meadowbank Stadium. I decided to quit. I jumped on the bus and headed back to the start.

I waited at the finish for Andrew to complete the race. Just before Andrew arrived, a loud cheer erupted in the stadium. A man in a diving bell outfit had entered the stadium. He made his way very slowly towards the finish line.

Andrew arrived at the stadium. He spotted Mr Diving Bell and decided to beat him to the finish line. He sprinted towards the line but just failed to catch the diver. How embarrassing. He was losing to a man in a diving bell outfit.

I congratulated Andrew, but I had to mock his inability to beat a man wearing an 80lb costume. This was slightly unfair as I subsequently discovered the diver had started the race seven days previously. Furthermore, it was such a cumbersome outfit to move in that he required a week to complete the course.

As Andrew went to get changed, I went to tell the organisers I had chosen to DNF. Does a DNF count if I never intended to start the race? Surely there should be a GLAT category for people who give a race a go despite no hope of completion. The God Loves A Trier status.

If you wonder about my nipples and who doesn't, I will get to them shortly.

Andrew

I don't remember why I entered the Edinburgh Marathon. I was running regularly, four to five times a week. Having just started a new job as a trainee lawyer, I would use my lunchtime to get out of the office and run four miles. Ha, I would think you can't chain me to a desk.

There were only a handful of people who were known as runners. One man invited me to run a 10k with him. On the way there, he explained how he would unstitch his trainers, cut the fabric and stitch them back together to get a lighter, more comfortable shoe. When I asked him how fast he expected to run the race, he explained in detail the exact second he was aiming for - and the likelihood of hitting it depending on the prevailing wind and humidity. He was a real runner. And by real runner, I mean a twat.

Another office runner had run the London Marathon the year before. How did you do that? I said. "One foot at a time," he said, "how else do you do it?". I loved his attitude, and I think it was him who inspired me to enter the Edinburgh Marathon because how hard could it be when it was just one foot at a time? If I'd only asked Mr Footstep, I would have known precisely how hard it would be – roughly 138,799 feet harder.

I tried to follow a marathon training programme with regular long runs and increasing distances each week to prepare for the race. That lasted about one week as I've never been good at consistent long runs. Instead, I would try and run my regular four-mile lunch run faster on the basis that if I could run part of the race faster then, when I slowed down, my average would still be okay. I mentioned I was a lawyer and not a scientist.

I managed one 20 mile run before the marathon, and I was feeling confident. Not only was I not drinking, but I'd also given up sweets. No chocolates, no cakes, no doughnuts, no sugar. It was horrible, and I've never done it again – you need a treat when you eat.

I can't remember who was meant to run with me. In my mind, Iain was always running it, but I also know that he never intended to finish it. I also didn't realise that he had been drinking – though I should have guessed when he had a bacon roll and a packet of yum yums for breakfast. You need a treat when you drink too.

I was excited to run. I was ready. But I also knew that, like Iain, I would be running on fumes. Though his were at the start, and mine would come when I hit 'The Wall'.

There'd been a lot of talk about The Wall before the race. I'd checked with Mr 138,799 Footsteps, and he explained how at some point, I would feel like I couldn't run any further, and no matter how much I tried, I wouldn't be able to push on. It was like hitting a wall as you would just come to a stop.

For me, that happened at mile 16, which goes to show the difference training can make. His wall was at mile 20 because he'd trained more. Mine was at mile 16 because I thought if I could run a half marathon in 1 hour 40 minutes, then I should double my time, and I'd be home in time to have a mid-morning kilo box of Quality Street.

Instead, at mile 16, I felt all energy leave my legs. I switched to a walk/run strategy of walking 10 miles after having already run 16 miles. I tried to run in the last mile when I saw a man in a diving costume ahead. After checking he was running by spotting his race number – you can't be too careful in Edin-burgh on a Sunday morning when stags are stumbling home – I tried to beat him with the thought that I couldn't lose to a deep-sea diver. Not knowing at this point that he'd started seven days ahead of me, I was gutted to lose the final sprint on the Meadowbank athletic track to what I thought was a man who managed to run faster than me in wellies and a snorkel.

My original aim was four hours, with the thought I should probably beat three hours 30 minutes as that would still be slower than two half marathons. But, in the end, I walked across the line in fours hours 11 minutes, behind the diver and just ahead of two rhinos.

My first marathon was done. All that was left was to pick up a chocolate muffin and then fall into two months of having no interest in ever running again as I was overcome by a tired-ness every time I even thought of running. However, if I had, I would never have clinched a world record 15 years later.

Iain

It's not a world record.

Andrew

Am I the fastest in the world?

Iain

We'll come back to this.

I decided I would try to do a marathon again, but I made an-other mistake. To explain this mistake, let me digress for a sec-ond and talk about another sport – Squash.

I play squash every week. I play the same man at the same time every week. And I lose every game. I occasionally win, but it is very rare. One year, I did not win a single match.

People ask me, "why do you play if you always lose?"

I play because the matches are competitive. The result feels like it could go either way, even though it only ever goes one way. However, eventually, I was tired of losing, so I asked myself – how do I stop losing? I need to stop giving away silly points. If I stop giving him points, then surely, I'd stop losing. I didn't. I kept losing. I lost every week until I realised I had asked myself the wrong question. I should have asked – how do I start winning?

My mentality was wrong. You can't win by trying not to lose. You win by trying to win. So, I came up with a plan to start playing with my head, not my hand. Think about where the shot should go. Play shots that will win the point. And, after making that change, I won more matches than I lost.

My opponent didn't take my wins well. He hated losing. It made him tetchy and annoyed. When his shot went wrong, he'd shout, yell and get distracted. What he shouted the most was: "IT'S NOT A TENNIS BALL!!!"

Which it wasn't. It was a squash ball. But he'd shout this because he played tennis more regularly than he played squash, and when he duffed a shot, he blamed it on the ball being the wrong ball in the wrong sport. Instead, he needed to change his mentality. He needed to shout: "IT IS A SQUASH BALL!". And having accepted it wasn't the ball that needed to change, he could improve his swing instead.

The lesson I have taken from squash is to respect what something is and not focus on what something is not.

This leads me to my second marathon DNF.

It was at the Fort William Marathon. This is an out and back course. I ran out, but I couldn't be bothered running back. It was a very dull route. It was a marathon route, and I should have respected the distance and not complained about something it was not – an exciting route.

I then signed up for another race…and I got another DNF.

It should be a DNS (Did Not Start). I'd entered the Berlin Marathon, and I trained well for it. I was confident that I would at last complete a marathon. There was only one issue. I had to fly to Berlin.

I hate flying. I have a fear of flying. Most people who fear flying hate taking off and landing, but I love those parts. I have a fear of the bit in-between take-off and landing. Every shake of the jet or stranger noise puts me on edge. I cannot relax, and I visualise falling out of the sky.

My fear was so bad this time that I decided not to fly. I did not make it to the start line. I didn't even make it to the airport.

Since then, I've created some strategies to cope with flying.

1.   I always book a window seat. I find looking out helps calm me down.

2.   I never fly by myself. If I have someone who is relying on me to go, then I can't pull out.

3.   I avoid early morning flights. I'm calmer if I've had a good night's sleep.

Now my only fear when flying is the fear of the race I'm flying to.

Andrew

I used to be scared of flying. Really scared. The kind of fear that makes you think twice about going to the airport. It was irrational. It was stupid. And I needed to find a cure, so I checked out a website that explained in forensic detail the purpose of every single knob, button, indicator and screen in the cockpit. Knowledge is power.

The website was meant to reassure the nervous flyer. Failsafe knobs are catching failsafe buttons catching failsafe indicators showing on failsafe screens. A pilot would need to be dead, dumb and blind not to know something was going wrong – and every button would have to fail before you ran out of buttons that could save you.

And, as yet another failsafe, you can be confident that your pilot is alive and is not dead, dumb and blind because they test for that in pilot school. Pretty much every airline insists on all of their pilots having eyes, mouths and ears. It's not the law, though, so, just as a precaution, before boarding a Ryanair flight, I'd check if the cockpit contains a kennel, just in case the pilot needs a spot for their dog.

And with this basic check complete, you can be confident that there are over 200 knobs, buttons, indicators and screens, making sure we don't fall from the sky. Who couldn't be impressed by all the measures in place to ensure we can fly safely while eating a free bag of nuts? It was a revelation. It cured my fear of flying because, after checking out the site, I realised one simple thing – NO MAN CAN REMEMBER ALL THOSE BUT-TONS! THERE ARE HUNDREDS OF THEM?!!! IT'S IMPOSSIBLE. HE'D NEED TO BE MR MEMORY! AND WHAT IF HE CAN'T GET THE INTERNET WHEN HE'S FLYING THE PLANE? HE SHOULDN'T BE CHECKING THE INTERNET WHEN FLYING! HIS PHONE SHOULD BE ON FLIGHT SAFE MODE!!!! OH GOD, WE'RE ALL GOING TO DIE!!!

And that's why I no longer fear flying because under no circumstances will I ever get on a plane again.

Iain

My fourth attempt at a marathon was the Tokyo marathon. One of my friends had moved to Tokyo, and he invited me over for the race.

He offered me a place to stay, which was great until I discovered he lived in a graveyard. He said Tokyo was very expensive to rent property in, so he could get a better property than he would typically have been able to afford by choosing to live in a place no one else wanted.

He liked to save money. One of the things he saved on was

food. He had worked out that rice was the most effective meal in terms of nutrients and cost. Therefore, he only eats rice. He would have rice with soya sauce and for breakfast and had rice with tomato sauce for lunch.

The money I saved on hotel bills by staying with him was spent booking a night at the Sheraton after the marathon. The hotel featured in the Bill Murray film 'Lost in Translation. I thought that I should have something to look forward to after the race that wasn't rice.

I do not remember much about the race other than it was a bit chilly and not very scenic. But instead of blaming it for reminding me of Fort William, what I did instead was concentrate on what I could control: my nipples. I told you I'd get around to discussing them eventually.

As I got near the finish, I felt a pain in my chest. My first thought was, "Am I having a heart attack?" so I did what all men do in the face of a medical issue. I ignored it. I stared ahead and concentrated on making it to the finish line.

As I crossed the finish line, the pain got worse. I put my hand to my chest: it felt damp. I looked down: my top was covered in blood. Where had the blood come from? I moved my hand around my chest. I felt my nipples. I screamed in agony. They were bleeding.

I realised that my decision to run the race in a Celtic FC football top was terrible. The thick heavy polyester of the top had chafed my nips like a cheese grater. I was practically nip-less. Now the panic set it. Maybe I'd need nip replacement surgery! Would Andrew donate one of his to me? If he didn't, where would I get one from? Should I get big or small ones? So many questions.

I did not have a replacement top, so I got the subway after the race and then walked to the Sheraton Hotel with my green, white, and blood-red top. I'm amazed they let me check-in. I phoned my friend for medical advice. He warned me that doctors in Japan were costly.

"What can I do? The bleeding won't stop?" I asked.

He said: "Have you tried soaking them in rice?"

I've not done a Marathon since then.

A few years ago, I attended a stand-up comedy course. At the end of the course, I performed a five-minute 'comedy' set.

At the end of the gig, a man came up to me to say, "I enjoyed that! You must let me know when you're performing again". I was pleased. I had only done one gig, but I'd already gained a fan. I told my fan that I had a gig booked for the following week at a comedy club. He promised to attend.

I was a bit nervous before the gig. After all, it was only my second ever gig, but before I went on, I looked out and saw my fan sitting in the front row. I thought to myself. At least there's one man here who'll laugh. I went out and performed my 'comedy'. My fan didn't laugh once. After the gig, I asked if he'd enjoyed it. "Not really." he replied, "I preferred your early stuff!". After that, I never saw him again.

I initially thought I would do another marathon after Tokyo. But every time I went to sign up for one, I found myself not very excited by it. The man in the comedy club was correct. It is the early stuff that is the best. The first time you run a 5K, a 10K or a half marathon is the one you remember the most.

Instead of signing up for a marathon, I decided to do the only running race I had never done before - an ultra-marathon.

I had not done one because I feared the distance and the loneliness of running for that far and long. But the only way to face fear is to deal with it. So I booked two ultramarathons for one year.

Andrew

Don't listen to him. Ultra-marathons are for idiots who think facing twice the fear is better than avoiding one. If you're scared of flying, book a train, don't book two flights. That's just twice the chance to die a horrible plummeting death.

Iain

My first race was the John Muir ultra-marathon. A 50K race that is relatively flat. I thought it would be an excellent introduction to long-distance running.

Anyone walking past my hotel room before the start of the race would have heard the following conversion between my wife and me.

"I've never done this before. Will it be sore?" I asked.

"I'm not sure, but I think lube will help," she replied.

A couple of seconds later, I scream. "Aaaargh!!! That's stings!"

"It's not that bad. Take it like a man!"

"Ooh, matron", as Kenneth Williams used to say in the Carry-On Film.

I'd applied a generous portion of chamois cream to my thighs, hoping it would protect my bits from chafing. However, I had been so worried about rubbing that I'd packed the cream into my race bag a few weeks previously to ensure I'd not forget it.

My pre-race aim was to run the first 30km, run/walk the next 10km and for the last 10km, just do whatever it took to finish under six hours.

The first 8km of the race is what I'd call the ultra-section. After that, it's just a marathon. And if I made it through the first 8km, then I knew I would definitely manage the rest of the route, as I'd proven I could do a marathon (once out of four attempts)

The 8km section was a little congested as the track we were all following was crowded with little room for overtaking. This was a good thing. It meant I could settle into a nice steady slow pace.

My only problem was that I regretted my choice of clothing. I had a waterproof jacket and a beanie on as rain had been forecast. However, there was no rain, and I was too warm wearing them. Which made me thankful there was a checkpoint at the 8km point. I dumped the clothes there.

After 8km, there was an excellent section through the fields near the town of Gullane. Many people have trouble pronouncing Gullane – is it pronounced GULLan or Gullane or Gillan or GILLane - but it's straightforward. Just say "that town with the weird name next to Aberlady". And if you don't know Aberlady, then just be thankful you don't live near Edinburgh.

Andrew

If you want to pronounce any Scottish place, just pronounce it like you're vomiting. Trust me, try it, pretend you're an alcoholic Scotsman, and everyone will think you're a native Sassenach. It works.

Iain

It was relatively flat and easy running through the town with the unpronounceable name, but the sky darkened, and the rain began as I left the town. Due to my earlier change of clothes, I now felt cold, wet and miserable. Which is a cliché to say. But it is a cliché because it's true. No one other than a seagull has ever been cold, wet and happy.

The rain wasn't heavy, but it was relentless. Luckily the route passed through a section of forest around Archerfield Estate. There was a food stop here. I was cold and wet (and, yes, miserable), but the positive news was that I had a chocolate brownie to eat. Delicious.

As we approached North Berwick, there were a few tiny hills. Hills that I usually wouldn't even call a hill. Most people would call them a slight bump in the road. I took one look at them and remembered what a friend of mine told me about hills in Ultras "Walk the hills!"

It was a relief to get to the halfway point, mainly because it had a roof so I could get out of the rain for a few minutes.

I had another chocolate brownie, and to be healthy, I also had a Twix. It's vegetarian, so it must be healthy! Correct??? Race advice always states you should race on what you train on. I eat Twix's the rest of the week, so I might as well eat them on race day too.

I felt great after the stop. This lasted about 100m when I got told by a marshal to run on the beach. Which was heavy thick sand, which made my legs feel very slow, but I barely noticed as I was on a Twix high. And then the rain stopped. Thank f**k for that.

After the beach, it's uphill past North Berwick Law. Again, it wasn't that hilly, and I usually wouldn't think twice about running it, but I still said to myself, "walk the hills!"

As I walked along, I overheard a male runner ask one of the volunteers.

"Do you have any Vaseline?"

The volunteer replied, "no," so he asked, "Do you think anyone ahead will have some? Please, God! My bits are on fire! It feels like my baws are trapped between two bits of sandpaper!"

He might not have said the last bit, but I could hear the fear of chafing in his voice. He should have packed cream in advance, like me.

Andrew

Good advice because if you hear someone say, "Stick it where the sun doesn't shine!" that's a threat, not an instruction. Also, you need to be careful about what you stick there because you will regret it if you get this wrong. Let me explain.

Around ten years ago, I took part in the Caledonian Challenge, a 54-mile walking challenge from Fort William to Loch Lomond and following the West Highland Way. You could run it but, as I said, I'm not an idiot, so I walked it. Does it count as an ultra-marathon if you walk it?

Iain

No – it doesn't count. You have to run it.

Or, in my case, run and walk it.

Andrew

I was walking with three teammates. It was our first challenge of this type, and we had no idea what we were doing.

We'd barely trained. We'd walked 20 miles along the Fife coastal path and, while using trekking poles to help us get used to using them in action, we were spotted by a local gang in Kirkcaldy. "Oi, yous!" They shouted, "'ave yous lost yer skis?".

Which was very funny – if you're not the prat trying to keep his dignity while walking with walking poles outside a chip shop in Kirkcaldy.

After that, we let training slide, and we thought we could just turn up at Fort William and wing it.

Big mistake. But not our biggest. Our biggest was not reading the instructions. If we had, we'd have spotted that long-distance walkers wear tight-fitting cycle shorts and not, I repeat NOT, ordinary boxers. Why? Let's just say one word – friction – and leave it at that. Or, if that doesn't help, let's just say one phrase – don't let Tarzan swing free – and leave it at that. Okay, okay, let's just spell it out. If you don't have tight-fitting shorts, then there's a whole lotta rubbing going on down there in a 54-mile walk — the kind of rubbing that a boy scout could use to start a fire.

By mile 40, we'd realised our mistake. We were the bow-legged walkers. If you'd seen us, you'd have shouted "Oi, lads, 'ave yous lost yer horses?". We looked like cowboys, felt like pillocks – until one of us had an idea.

"We've got sun-cream!" He said.

"So?"

"It's a lubricant, isn't it?"

"Is it?"

"Well, it's wet."

And, with that rigorous debate over, three of the four of us were hiding behind a bush, trousers round our ankles and applying sun-cream to areas that frankly the sun had only ever shined out of.

Five minutes later, no longer bow-legged: "This is BRILLIANT!"

And it was.

For five more minutes. Then the first cry went up.

"AAAAAAAAAAAAAARRRRRRRRRRRRRGGGGGGGGGGG-GGGGHHHHHHH."

The second cry went up.

"EEEEEEEEEEEEEEEEEEKKKKKKKKKKKKKKKKKKKK."

The third cry went up.

"JAAAAAAAAAAAYYYYYYYYYY-YZZZZZZZZZZZUUUUUUSSSSCCCCCCHHHHHRRRIIISSSSTT-TTT!"

Then we all fell down.

It was agony. It turns out sun cream is not a lubricant at all. It was chilli oil. There was heat and pain in places that only a naked Mexican who's sat on a red hot burrito will ever experience.

"AAAAAAAAAAAAAARRRRRRRRRRRRRRGGGGGGGGGGG-GGGGHHHHHHH."

But it wasn't the worst thing to happen that day. It turns out one of us had an even smarter (dumber) idea. He'd said he didn't need to use the cream; however, it was only after the race that we found out why.

He'd wrapped zinc oxide tape around his toes to prevent chafing and blistering. Then, in a move that only the Darwin Awards can appreciate, he decided to use the leftover tape on other parts of his body that might be subject to chafing.

He, and, well, let me be delicate about it, had wrapped, um, Tarzan's hanging baskets in tape. And it worked: he didn't feel a thing for the entire race. He was very smug until he got home. Then he realised that the only way to take the tape off was to rip it off. And when it was ripped off, it took everything with it. Every little and not so little hair. He spent three hours in the bath, hoping the tape would soak and fall off naturally.

It didn't.

He had no choice. He had to let it rip. He had smooth toes. And Tarzan was bald.

"AAAAAARRRRRRRRGGGGGGGGHHHHHHHH!!!!!!!!!!!!"

He never used zinc oxide again.

Iain

I was fine. I had my lube, and after the hill, I headed into a pleasant forest section that looped around a small loch. At one point, I spotted some gravestones in the trees. I thought, "That's a strange place to be buried", but I then noticed the names of the graves – Mr Tiddles III, Dwayne Mousecatcher, and Rex. I hope it was a pet cemetery and not one for real people. Though if it was for real people, I'm impressed that Mr Tiddles named his son Mr Tiddles II and then he thought, "I need to keep this name going" and named his son Mr Tiddles III

Onwards from the cemetery, the course headed slightly downhill through fields. It seemed to be a new path as the track and fencing alongside it seemed to have just been put up. I decided to have another Twix that I'd saved from earlier. You can never have too many bars of Twix.

The last hill was again minor, but it was a 'walk the hill' hill.

At 40K, my legs were sore and tired. I switched to walking a couple of 100m every time I completed a kilometre.

As I entered the last 5K, the sun came out

. I decided to walk the flat and enjoyed a nice, paced walk to the finish. Occasionally, a runner would pass and say, "Sorry! I'm just a relay runner." to explain why they looked so fresh when I didn't.

At the end of the race, I overheard a woman say to her friend: "Nooo! I don't believe it. I went to stop my watch, and it didn't stop, it started! I must not have pressed start at the beginning of the race."

This is annoying because everyone knows Strava kudos does not count if you manually create your activity. You need to have GPS tracking, or it did not happen.

I pressed stop on my GPS watch as I crossed the finish line. I'd finished my first 50K race. I looked at my watch to confirm it. It said I'd only done 49.8K! It says a lot about how hard the race was (for me) that I had absolutely no desire to walk another 200 metres to get the distance to 50k.

The race finish line was near a farm. As I headed to my car, I overheard two runners having an argument.

Runner 1: It was a llama

Runner 2: It was an alpaca!

Runner 1: No! It was a llama!

Runner 2: Look, mate! If there's one thing I know, it's alpacas. It's a fucking alpaca!

Runner 1: F**koff! It's a llama. You're talking out your arse.

Runner 2: Stick the llama up your arse!

It was an alpaca. I know this because I Googled it after the race. I also spotted the name of the farm. Bob's Alpaca farm.

Whoever said running is a stress reliever has obviously never felt passionate about llamas and alpacas.

Andrew

Iain saw an exotic animal. I saw a ghost. It wasn't an actual ghost because the man was very much alive, just not anywhere near where I saw him.

After 20 miles of walking, my feet had given up. I couldn't move a foot without my boots pinching my toes with all the gentleness of an elephant giving a massage. I wanted to quit. But I couldn't. I was in the middle of nowhere. I was on my own, my teammates having abandoned me, and I was 6 miles from any road where I could cadge a lift. I sat down. I gave up. And then it started to rain.

As I tried to rouse myself to keep walking, I could see and hear a man approach me along the trail. My luck was in because this man was the event organiser. I recognised him from videos sent before the race to share tips and preparation.

He smiled at me. "Keep going," he said, "you can do it!".

And if the man in the video thought I could do it, then I wasn't going to disappoint. I got up. He patted me on the back, and I shuffled on for another three hours to complete those final six miles.

When I crossed the finish line, I saw him again handing out medals. When I handed out mine, I thanked him and told him that his words had inspired me to finish. He looked at me puzzled and said, "I've been here the entire time." And, when I looked back, I did think it was strange he was riding a pink giraffe, but it wasn't until then that I knew for sure that I'd hallucinated the whole thing.

That's why you don't take part in ultra-marathons. On the other hand, no one's ever lost their mind in the middle of a 5k fun run.

Iain

My second ultra was later the same year. The Devil O' The Highlands - a 42-mile point to point race along the West Highland Way from Tyndrum to Fort William.

I've always wanted to do the race for no other reason than the name sounded exciting. Who wouldn't want to race the Devil?

At the start of the race, a woman next to me said. "I've not trained for this" I looked at her. She looked very fit. She looked like she should be on an advert for a gym as an example of what would happen if you went to the gym and trained every day for a year.

She then said, "I've done nothing since The Highland Fling (a 53-mile ultra)... other than three marathons and loops of Glencoe every morning before work. I don't know if I'll be able to do this."

If she did not think she could do it, then I was in trouble, as I had not done any marathons, and the only loop I do in the morning is a breakfast bowl of Honey Nut loops.

Oh well – there was nothing more I could do. At least I'd made it to the start line fit and healthy. I had a plan that I was confident would get me to the end of the course.

I would run the first 10km to Check Point 1 in Bridge of Orchy in 60 minutes. Then, run the 10 miles to CP2 in Glencoe in two hours. Next, run the (hilly) 8 miles to Kinlochleven in two hours and then run/walk the rest of the way to Fort William in four to five hours.

I just had to trust the plan...

The first part of the race runs past the Toblerone-Esque Ben Dorain. Its distinctive triangular shape looks like a... Toblerone. It's a popular hill that a lot of people climb. I've only done it once. It was a cloudy, wet day with no view from the top. When I got back down, a man asked me, "did you get to the top?"

I replied, "yes.", as this was not Kilimanjaro all over again.

He said, "the second cairn?"

I replied, "what second cairn?"

"The second cairn is the real top," he said, "the first one is a false top."

Oh well. It was Kilimanjaro all over again, but at least I'd reached my top...

My plan was to run the first section easy. Don't run past anyone; just stay at the pace of the group. That plan lasted until the first slight incline when lots of folks started walking. I suspect they were following a 'walk the climbs, run the flats/downhills' plan, but it seemed too early for that, so I kept running and overtook them all.

I thought the section was relatively flat, but afterwards, I noticed one of my mile splits was a six-minute mile pace. There must have been a downhill section that I overlooked. I blame the early start. I was still half asleep.

There's a road crossing at Bridge of Orchy manned by volunteers stopping the traffic. I was amazed I recognised one of them. I'd been at Uni with him but hadn't seen him in years.

It's a very Scottish thing to say what something is not rather than what something is. Ask a Scotsman what the weather is like on a sunny day, and instead of replying "it is sunny", he will say, "it's not raining". Ask a Scotsman how an event has gone. Instead of saying "it was good", he'll say, "it wasn't shite".

I realised this after he shouted, "how are you" and I replied, "I'm not bad."

Why didn't I just say I'm good? I was good. I reached the CP in just over an hour. Right on schedule.

I'd only ever done the section from Bridge of Orchy to Glencoe once, and it was during a night walk. It was pitch dark, and I didn't see a thing. I was looking forward to seeing the route in daylight.

There was a kit check as soon as I left CP1 and then the first hill of the day. I walked most of it to conserve energy. After that, the route was a bit dull and samey. Lots of moors. It turns out I hadn't missed much by not seeing this section previously.

Andrew

At this point, I got up, had breakfast and started driving to CP2. As I'd agreed to meet Iain there.

Iain

After a few miles, I got bored of the view, so I tried to listen to a podcast, but my hands were so sweaty my touch screen phone wouldn't respond to my touch. I tried wiping it on my clothes, but everything I had was either damp or sweaty, so it didn't help. After the race, I realised I didn't need to use my hands; I could have just said, "Siri! Play music."

The midges were terrible on this section. Thankfully I grew up in the Western Isles. Mainland midges are just a minor inconvenience compared to the flesh-eating flying monsters I've experienced at home.

I reached Glen Coe just after 0900. Thankfully, my support team were there as I'd told them to get me at 0930. I was a bit quicker than I initially thought. I picked up some food and refilled my bottles before heading off.

Andrew

By this point, Iain had almost run a marathon. This is why

ultramarathons are stupid. Why run a marathon when you could get out of bed at a normal time and do anything else?!?! And then you still have to run another marathon?!?

Iain

The following section was the one I was looking forward to the most. If asked to describe the next bit, I would have to say, "it's not flat". The first significant climb is called the Devils Staircase.

The number 666 is commonly associated with the Devil, but did you know the number 33 is associated with God? The reason why:

AMEN in numeric form is $1+13+5+14=33.33$ degrees latitude, and 33 degrees longitude is where angels are supposed to have fallen to earth. And 33 Celsius was how hot it got on this section. It was at that point I exclaimed, "OH MY GOD! It is so hot!"

The Devil O' The Highlands race was aptly named because it was the air temperature that day was hot as hell. The temperature got hotter and hotter as I approached the Devils Staircase. There was no wind to cool me down, which made the climb more challenging than it would normally be. At the top, a man dressed as the Devil was handing out Jelly Babies. I hope it was fancy dress. I took a jelly baby. I may have sold my soul in the process, I'm not sure. Unfortunately, I didn't have a chance to check the terms and conditions for taking a sweetie.

The view from the top of the Staircase was beautiful. I was not the only person who thought that. A man behind me (who had a booming voice) said/shouted:

"THIS IS BEAUTIFUL!"

Yes, it is. Thanks for pointing it out. Then 10 seconds later…

"WHAT A VIEW"

Thanks again. I would not have noticed unless you had said something. Then ten seconds later.

"STUNNING!"

It still was. It hasn't changed in the last 10 seconds!

Then 10 seconds later...

"AMAZING!"

Please be quiet! Then 10 seconds later.

"GLORIOUS!"

Did someone buy him a thesaurus for Christmas!

Then 10 seconds later... SILENCE. Thankfully, he must have run out of words. His thesaurus must be the abridged version. I took in the view and enjoyed the peace and quiet until he boomed: " THIS IS BEAUTIFUL!" Then 10 seconds later... "WHAT A VIEW!" He must have been stuck on a loop. And not a nice one, like a Honey Nut loop.

At this point, I slowed down and let him run on ahead as I couldn't bear listening to him holler for the whole race about how beautiful the course was.

I wonder how his wife puts up with it: she must serve his diner, and then he'll start going: "THIS IS DELICIOUS... TASTY... SCRUMMY... THIS IS DELICIOUS...TASTY..."

From the top, it was mostly downhill to Kinlochleven. I enjoyed this section as the views were great, and the running was easy, although, towards the end of the run, I felt a slight pain in my left leg. I ignored it and hoped it would clear up once I was on flatter terrain. Just before the finish, I heard someone sing, "Woah, we're halfway there!" which worried me as I was sure we were two-thirds of the way there. They then sang, "Woah, livin' on a prayer!". Thankfully it wasn't a runner proclaiming the distance but a walker playing Bon Jovi very loudly from a stereo strapped to his rucksack. He was walking with folks who, I hope, all loved Bon Jovi too.

I reached Kinlochleven about twenty minutes slower than

planned, but I was happy to have got this far in good time. Only 15 miles to go. I changed my clothes and shoes at CP3. It's incredible what a difference a fresh pair of socks makes. My wife joined me as a support runner/walker. She had been due to race but had to drop out due to injury.

Andrew

I left after this checkpoint. Went home. Went out on the bike. Had my dinner and started watching a movie all before he finished. Ultras are for dafties!

Iain

Although I'm not the most talkative or appreciative person at events, it was good to have company. I switch to a "just get it done" mode that I struggle to shake off until an event is over. It's a mental strength that helps with endurance races but probably doesn't help my marriage. Thankfully, she forgave me afterwards.

I slathered on suntan lotion, and then we headed out. I put a bottle of Lucozade and a can of coke in my backpack, so I could treat myself later. The climb out of CP3 to CP4 is the longest climb of the day. It's not hard, but in the heat, it was a slog.

I decided it was too hot to run, so I fast-walked this section... and the next section– in fact, I didn't run again until 100m from the finish.

It was probably the most beautiful part of the course. It was very peaceful walking through the valleys. Occasionally we would pass a runner or walker, but mostly it was just the two of us plodding along.

The checkpoint seemed to be in the middle of nowhere. It might have been near civilisation, but it was tough to tell. I refilled my water bottle and had a celebratory coke. Only 10K to go

I felt good leaving CP4, and I was confident of finishing. The route was undulating for a few miles. Some single-track roads in which it would be easy to trip over rough terrain. As one man discovered when he jogged past and then tripped over a tree root 20m later. He jumped up unhurt, but he looked a bit embarrassed.

A lot of this section was spent staring at Ben Nevis. It seemed so close, but despite walking on and on, it felt we'd never get there.

I've climbed it a couple of times, but I've never been seen it on a day as clear as this.

One man asked me, "is that the hill we have to go up at the end?". He'd heard there was a hill right at the finish. I said yes, even though it wasn't the hill. He looked terrified and ran off. I shouted that I was only joking, but I'm not sure he heard me.

As we reached the finish line. I decided to jog a little so the finish photo would look like I had run it all.

I crossed the finish line in 9hr 40min-ish. My aim had been below nine hours, so I was pleased to not be too far off it. The hot day meant it was an achievement just to finish.

I picked up some tasty hot food and sat down for the first time since 5am.

Andrew

Iain might think he can beat me running by running two ultra-marathons when I've run none. But there are many different records. Some will never be defeated. You can't be the first person on the moon when Neil Armstrong got there first. Nor can you climb Everest when Edmund Hillary did it over sixty-five years ago. Some records last.

Others are less serious. If you read the Guinness Book of World Records, you'll find a record for the world's longest fingernails. A world record that literally doesn't require you to lift a finger – in case you break a nail.

Or how about Etibar Elchyev, who took the title for 'Most spoons balanced on a human body by balancing 50 spoons. He'd have balanced more, but Sharon from accounts wanted to make a cup of tea, and he ran out.

You'd think he'd have balanced more if he'd used teaspoons?!

Or, worse, instead of spoons. How about balancing bees? Chinese beekeeper, She Ping covered his body with 330,000 bees. Honey, I'm home!

I think I'll stick to cutlery.

But as records become devalued – you cannot compare spoons and bees with standing on the moon – we each have the opportunity to find our own records. If you join Strava, you too can be a record-breaker as every route or part of routes is carefully broken down into segments to create mini record opportunities. For example, do you want to be the fastest person to run along your street? Then create a segment and run faster than anyone else running along with it. Or, if you can't run fast, at least walk it while carrying 330,000 bees and claim the record for the fastest person to be stung to death on your street.

Despite how easy it is to claim a record, records still matter. Or at least they do to me. We want to know who's the fastest, who's the strongest, who's the most likely to open a cafe and not need cutlery. And I want to know who's the fastest at running the only hill in Stornoway: The War Memorial.

It's not the steepest or longest or hardest climb, but it does provide a few minutes of running to take you to a vantage point over the whole of Stornoway and out to the mainland.

And for the last few years, I've been trying to be the fastest to run up it. It's my Everest, moon and jumbo onion (another official world record).

How do you like dem onions?

And two weeks later, I almost managed it. I almost had my

onion.

The weather was poor. The wind was in the wrong direction. I didn't even think I was running hard enough to make an attempt on the record when I got home, checked Strava, and, blimey, I was the second-fastest in the world.

Which is the one record no one wants – no one wants to be second! What's the point of having 49 spoons on your body when the man up the road has 50?!

In 2018 and 2019, I went all out for the record. I was going to run like 330,000 bees were chasing me, and this record would be mine - or I'd cry like a man who just peeled the world's largest onion.

Iain

Andrew told me about the record. I ran the segment. A Todd became the fastest in the world, but it was not Andrew. It was me.

Andrew

What Iain fails to mention is that he cheated. He got his wife to hold a gate open. The gate is about halfway along the route, and I've always had to open it myself. This was dope-gating.

Iain

Haterz gonna hate.

Andrew

And I couldn't let him get away with it. Every time I went home, I would try again, and finally, finally, finally, I conquered the War Memorial segment on Strava to become the fastest person in the world to climb Stornoway's highest spot.

It almost didn't happen. First, when Iain checked the top ten, it turned out that another competitor had secretly conquered the top spot just three weeks before. No longer was Iain the fastest man in the world (up the War Memorial); another had sneaked in under the radar and stolen the top spot. I needed to not only run faster than Iain but also now, Michael, who was taking the Micky.

I was planning to attempt a run on Boxing Day but, when we went out a few days before, Iain wanted to give it a go. I wasn't up for it. I felt tired and was only wanting an easy run around the Castle Grounds. But, after he said to give it a go, I thought it would be good practice for the 'real' attempt later in the week.

There was no wind, so I thought this run would be slower. How was I meant to run fast if I didn't have a helping push? So, I tried running fast, but not necessarily as fast as I could. This was just practice anyway.

I didn't even check the time when I got home. I thought there was no point as it would only show how much faster I would need to go.

But, when I did, all I can say is... HAIL TO THE KING, BABY!

Transition Three: Massage

Andrew

My clothes are neatly folded, and I'm lying face-down wearing nothing but my pants. There is an awkward silence as a pretty young girl in immaculate make-up considers the word "groin".

It's at this point I regret my choice of Bugs Bunny boxers. Her eyes flick down, and I feel less than magnificent.

It's not uncomfortable. This is not my first massage, but it is my first with a woman.

Typically, it's Steve the Physio. Steve the Physio is practical. Steve the Physio doesn't do small talk. "Groin?" he asks. And when I nod, he roughly pulls my legs apart and, before going to work, sternly tells me to "Cup the balls, and pull them back".

This is not a phrase I've ever had to use, not that it would fit any other social situation.

"Andrew, can you pass the English mustard?"

"First, cup the balls, and pull them back!"

"Andrew, do you have any spare change for the bus?"

"FIRST, cup the BALLS! And pull them back!"

"Andrew, is this extended flight of fantasy becoming laboured?"

"CUP THE BALLS AND PULL THEM BACK!"

But Steve the Physio is on holiday, and last week I was presented with the slim and attractive Muriel. The thought of asking her to work the groin is making me feel ever so uncomfortable. Not that it should. She's a professional; I'm a customer. This is an NHS-approved physiotherapy clinic, not a cat-house (second only to a duck-house in dodgy MP expense claims).

I think of saying nothing. Saying nothing is okay during a massage. No one expects a running commentary or political discussion. Small talk is fine. In fact, anything is fine, except for "oooooh!", "aaaaaahhhh!" and "just a lit bit".

But my inner thigh has tightened and, if I am to resume running, I need her fingers to work their magic. So, when she approaches, when she lays her gentle hands upon my back and asks, "According to Steve, it's normally your groin that's the problem, is that right?"

I don't say: "Yes if by a problem you mean it's too big!".

Instead, I nod, glad that she has gotten the G-word out of the way. I can relax safe in the knowledge that I'm not going to embarrass myself by making some well-intended but sexually sounding overtone to this young girl. Everything is going to be okay.

Until she says, "So, where should we start?"

And I say, without thinking: "Cup the balls and pull them back!"

PART 3

CHAPTER EIGHT: TRIATHLON

Iain

In September 2008, I joined the Royal Bank of Scotland. My first day was fantastic. I met my teammates, I got taken out for lunch, and we all went to a bar and got drunk in the evening.

Even better, my manager paid for the lunch and all the evening's drink using his corporate credit card. As I went to sleep that night, I thought how lucky I was to have such a great job.

My second day wasn't as good – the bank collapsed due to the financial crash.

Later that day, my manager had to hand back his corporate credit card. There was to be no more lunches or drinks paid for by RBS.

I don't think the financial crisis was my fault, but I can't be sure: I was very drunk on my first day.

The only good thing that came out of my time at RBS was discovering triathlons. One day, an RBS project manager told me about a race he'd entered – the Edinburgh New Year's Day Triathlon. First, a 400m swim in a pool, then three laps on a bike of Arthur's Seat, finishing with one lap running around Arthurs Seat.

It sounded great, so I signed up. I then realised I hadn't swum since school. I should have practised swimming before the event, but I ignored it like all men faced with a complex problem. I'm not sure I took any of the event seriously. This is what I wrote on Facebook the night before the race: "Iain M Todd is going to play a game called how much beer can he drink and still be able to do a triathlon the next day".

At 3 am, five hours before the start of the race, I was still playing that game, and I had a very high score. It is fair to say my pre-race fueling strategy was flawed. I woke up very hungover, but I made it to the start.

The swim was eight laps of the commonwealth pool. I used the breaststroke for all of them. I remember thinking, "this is the furthest I've ever swum", and that was at the end of lap one. Every metre after that was a new record.

The bike was worse. I had an old mountain bike. Thankfully I was not breathalysed before hitting the road. Unfortunately, my bike broke on lap one. Everyone passed me as I tried to fix it. I eventually got it working, and I made it round slowly.

My drinking caught up with me on the run. I threw up at the start, the middle and the end of the lap. I eventually finished last.

But that wasn't the worst part of the day. Earlier, after the swim, I went to the changing room to use the hairdryer instead of going to the bike transition area. I wasn't going to go out on New Year's Day in Scotland with wet hair. I'd catch a cold.

As I was blow-drying my hair, the project manager from RBS saw me. He assumed I must have finished. He strode over to me and asked how my race had gone. I replied that I was currently doing it. He looked appalled and strode off.

It was at this point I learnt that some people race to compete and some race to complete.

That day I completed...just.

Andrew

I was also at the Edinburgh race. I came second last. At least I beat Iain.

It wasn't my first triathlon. That happened in London. Roughly the same time as when the famous chef Gordon Ramsay tried to kill me.

I'd booked Sunday lunch at his then three Michelin star restaurant at Claridge's. When I booked it, I said, "no nuts – I'm allergic". When I arrived, the Maître D asked if I had any allergies. I said, "yes, nuts." He said, "we'll make sure there are no nuts on the plate." And then he served me hazelnuts as part of my starter. Then more nuts from my main course. And then, despite twice saying, "I don't eat nuts", I was served a dessert with some crunchy bits artistically scattered over the top. "Are those nuts?" I asked. The waiter said, "no", then looked at them again. "I'll ask the chef," and he took away the plate – and came back without the crunchy 'nutty' bits...

Afterwards, I wrote to Gordon Ramsay to complain. The big man himself wrote back. "I'm very sorry that..." and then the letter went blank for a half-page before "yours sincerely, signed Gordon Ramsay".

And all I could think was how many complaints does he get that he doesn't even read the complaints letters to check what he's apologising for? But it did give me the perfect space to write my own apology in the space he'd left.

"I'm very sorry that I am a big angry sweary bollock monster, yours sincerely, signed Gordon Ramsay."

Thanks, Gordon.

Which is a bit harsh. I do like Gordon Ramsay because he got me into triathlons. He was competing in the first triathlon I tried. In fact, he was only a couple of bikes away in transition. And I remember reading that he used to get up at 5am to train, and I thought, "well, if he can do it at 5am, then it'll be easy for me as I can run during the day!".

I was so, so wrong.

I was working in London at the time, and I'd entered the London Triathlon. I'd joined as a team, as I couldn't understand why anyone would want to take part in the whole thing. I agreed to run, and that was more than enough for me. My friend, Graham, would swim, and a girl we knew from work, Sally, would cycle. It seems simple. He'd swim. She'd ride. I'd run. What could go wrong?

First, Graham had never swum outside. He was a strong swimmer. He had swum for his university, but only ever in a pool. He borrowed a wet suit and was near the front when he came out of the water. Then a man told him, "You need to take your wetsuit off".

“What do you mean?” He asked.

"You need to strip out your wetsuit and carry it to transition".

“But I don’t have any trunks on!”

It hadn’t occurred to him that he might need to wear swim trunks. He thought a wet suit was enough.

"But you were borrowing it," I said later. "Did you not want to wear trunks for a borrowed wetsuit?"

“I never thought about it,” he said.

“Clearly!”

I watched in transition as he went from first to near the last, arguing with the race marshal about how much of the wetsuit he could keep on while not disqualifying himself from the race. Eventually, with legs pulled up and top pulled down and waddling towards us in what now looked like the Michelin Man’s rubber pants, we started the bike race – and Sally admitted she’d never ridden a bike before in the UK.

She was South African, so that was okay; she knew how to ride on the left-hand side of the road. But she'd been in the UK for four years, so was admitting that she hadn't trained at all. Not even to sit on her bike. A ladies bike. With side saddle and all.

We went from near last to last.

And then I ran. The easy part. Though by this point, Gordon Ramsay had gone home.

I ran. And I ran. And I kept going faster, thinking, "I can catch up with the man in second last place".

And then I came back to transition and thought: "that was quick, and I'm glad this is over". Only to find that I was running laps and had three more laps to run. D'oh!

I hadn't checked the course at all.

We didn't rise through the ranks; I started last and finished last.

Then, to cap it off, I found out the London Underground wouldn't let bikes on the Tube, and I had to cycle Sally's bike all the way back from Canary Wharf to West Hampstead because Sally swore never to ride again.

And I got lost and ended up in Wembley.

But, because Gordon Ramsay was doing it, we swore (no pun intended) to come back the following year and do it right because "if that twat off the telly can do it, then we can do it too."

Iain

After my first triathlon, I had no intention of doing one ever again, but then I spotted a video on YouTube. It was called "Norseman 2012 – Breaking Barriers".

I was intrigued by the image of people wearing wetsuits standing at the back of a ferry. I wasn't sure why they were there or what they were doing, but I was wanted to know more about it.

The video starts with people being interviewed. They are asked how they felt about the jump. I thought, what jump? The folk in the video seemed scared of it. I watched as the video showed athletes entering a ferry in the middle of the night. The ferry then pulls away from the harbour and heads out to a fjord.

It then cuts to a drone shot of the ferry. A couple of hundred yellow capped, wetsuited athletes are standing on the car deck of the ferry. The back of the car deck opens. Then athletes start jumping into the water. Wow – this looks amazing! What was this?

I've spent years travelling on a ferry between the Scottish mainland and my parent's home in the Western Isles. Sometimes the journey was so dull I've thought of jumping off just to liven up the trip. But this was something different. These people didn't have a death wish. I was transfixed. The video went on. It showed the athletes swimming back to shore, it showed them biking through beautiful Norwegian scenery, and finally, it showed the pain and glory of athletes running to the top of a mountain.

I didn't understand what I'd seen. I wasn't even aware of the distances involved, but I was determined to do this race.

I then remembered, as you might have gathered from the previous chapters, I'm not a great swimmer or biker or runner. So it wasn't a good start.

I also had one other concern. Previously, when I'd become obsessed by a race. I'd trained for it to the detriment of different aspects of my life. However, I was determined to do the race right. I'd learn to do triathlons properly, and I'd make sure that when taking part, it wouldn't interfere with any other area of my life - all triathlon and no play would make Iain a dull boy.

I started by researching what a triathlon is. I discovered they come in different lengths and different types.

A sprint triathlon is 750 meter swim / 20 kilometre bike / 5 km run. A Standard or Olympic distance triathlon is a 1.5 kilometre swim / 40km bike / 10 km run. A medium-distance triathlon is a 1.9 kilometre swim / 90 km bike / 21.1 km run. An Ironman or long-distance triathlon is a 3.8 kilometre swim / 180.2 km bike / 42.2 km run

After reading the distances required, I decided I would never take part in an Ironman distance triathlon. Why would anyone want to do that distance? It sounded impossible.

I then researched what Norseman was. What a relief – I discovered it was not an Ironman. Oh...wait a sec. It said it was an Extreme Triathlon. Was that good or bad? Hopefully, it meant it was extremely short.

It wasn't. It was an Ironman distance, but each part was extreme, e.g. the swim is extremely cold, the bike and run routes are extremely high, have extremely bad weather and can be extremely cold. This did not sound like fun. It sounded extreme. It was well named.

A race report said doing Norseman was Type 2 fun. I thought the only thing that comes in types 1, 2 or 3 is diabetes. Categorising fun does seem to remove the fun from fun.

'Type 1 Fun' is fun that you experience whilst doing an activity, and once you've finished it, you still think of it as fun. For example, a post-race pint of beer is fun. You'll have fun drinking it, and you'll never regret it afterwards.

'Type 2 Fun' is fun that doesn't feel like fun whilst you are doing it, but afterwards, you'll be glad you did it. For example, if you don't go for a pint before a race, you might miss out on the fun, but when you wake up fresh the next day, you'll be glad you didn't.

'Type 3 Fun' is fun that is miserable whilst you do it, and afterwards, you'll wish you hadn't done it. This is when you go for a pint before a race and then have another and another...the next day, you race with a hangover. You'll hate it whilst doing it, and afterwards, you'll wish you hadn't done it.

The interesting thing about Type 3 Fun is that it can become Type 2 Fun over time because you might forget how miserable you felt and might actually be glad you did the race.

Most fun experts seem to stop at three types. I'd argue there is a fourth type. Type 4 Fun is fun at the time, but afterwards, you'll regret it. Which sums up any time I've eaten a Krispy Kreme.

I had to accept that Norseman would not be fun...until I finished it. After that, it would be Type 2 fun.

But to finish it, I would first have to enter some shorter, non-extreme triathlons. But I wouldn't tell Andrew that Norseman was my dream. Because then I wouldn't fail. If no one knew about it, then they wouldn't know if I failed. But I did want help, so I convinced him to do a triathlon. We decided to start at the beginning and attempt a sprint race.

Andrew

I had no interest in taking part in a triathlon. I loved running and cycling, but swimming, like home economics and the measles, was something you left behind when you left school. Never mind jumping from a ferry. That wasn't type 1, 2, 3 or 4 fun. That was an ongoing incident requiring an emergency helicopter, a coast guard, and a winch.

Yet when Iain said, "do you want to take part in a triathlon?" I said yes because I had no idea what I was agreeing to, so I had no reason to say no. It's the same reason that Columbus discovered America by trying to reach India by sailing east from Spain and not west. I didn't know what I was about to discover.

Iain

Bishopbriggs Triathlon has a reputation as one of the best beginner-friendly triathlon races in Scotland.

My preparation for the race didn't go well. I didn't realise I had to be there early to put the bike into transition. By the time I arrived, the official car park was full. I managed to get a car parking space in a side street, but I didn't write down the street's name. I wouldn't realise until later that Bishopbriggs has a lot of very similar-looking side streets.

I'd like to say the swim went smoother than my parking, but I made some rookie errors:

I underestimated my swim time. When entering the event, I had to give a predicted time for the swim. I guessed and added a couple of minutes to make sure I wasn't in a fast lane.

My estimate was too slow. I was much faster than everyone else in the lane. I should have realised I wasn't among fast swimmer when everyone arrived wearing rubber rings and snorkels.

Outside, the weather had been dry when I placed them in transition but, during the swim, it had rained, and all my stuff was wet. I should have put a plastic waterproof bag over them to keep the rain off. My bike seat was soaking wet. If I'd put a plastic bag over it, then I would have enjoyed a nice dry seat instead of a "wet Andrew", which is my code for a soaking wet arse.

Finally, my biggest mistake was that I'd put my safety pins through the front and back of my cycle top, preventing me from getting into the top. I had to undo all the pins. Put the top on and then tack on the number. Ever since this, I've used a race number belt.

I headed out onto the bike course. There were many bikes on the course, from mountain bikes to hybrids to full-on time trial-specific machines. Maybe triathlons shouldn't be just about age group results but about how much was spent on the bike. But then again, I saw one man on a hybrid race past a man on his time trial bike. Maybe it is about how hard people train.

The bike route was five laps of a short course. It was boring. Something not mentioned in most triathlon reports is that some courses can be exceedingly dull. It wasn't even scenic.

The loop passed a waste disposal centre and an environmental health storage facility. Since then, I've been very careful to only sign up for races that take place in lovely places or at least not in sight of a garbage facility.

I managed to rack my bike successfully and head out for the run. The run was the first time I'd ever seen a spray can be used as a course feature. After running 2km, I had to run around a spray can, which was placed in the middle of a path, back to the start. I thought, why don't they just spray the ground instead of putting the can there?

The last kilometre was along a muddy path, and, annoyingly, I had on new trainers. I abandoned running quickly and instead ran cleanly as I gingerly avoided every bit of mud. That was my excuse for my slow run time.

I was happy the race was complete. I wasn't last, so I had improved since my Edinburgh Triathlon debut.

I collected all my stuff, but I'd forgotten where the car was parked; I had to spend twenty minutes on my bike, exploring the back streets of Bishopbriggs, trying to find it.

The next challenge was to attempt a standard distance race

Andrew

"Water, water everywhere, nor any drop to drink…"

… because I can see a shopping trolley, a thin layer of green slime and an alkie having a piss behind a bin.

The River Clyde that splits Glasgow in half like a razor through a throat is not a river you swim in, not unless you have a radiation suit, a snorkel and a bath of hydrochloric acid to scrub yourself clean. The River Dee, on the other hand, splits Chester apart like a blue ribbon. It's clean, genteel and demands that you dip more than your toes into it. It's a proper river, unlike the Clyde, which, to Glaswegians, is less a river and more a naturally occurring accessory to murder.

Until I started entering triathlons, I would never have thought of swimming in any river. I could barely swim in a swimming pool. But, after accepting Iain's challenge to take part in a triathlon, I knew I would have to learn to swim 'proper' as I only knew the breaststroke.

They say that before you walk, you should learn to crawl, but, for swimming, before you crawl, you need to learn how to drown. Repeatedly. I spent three months just learning to breathe out of the side of my mouth without swallowing half of the pool. It was slow going, but I kept practising and followed my coach's instructions to the letter. Unfortunately, that letter was W for "wrong."

My couch was Iain, and while he should have been teaching me my ABC's he missed out on the basics and had me working on a swim shape that made me look like an epileptic squid. You're meant to glide through the water. I sunk.

Lesson: don't appoint a 'coach' who only learnt to swim the week before you.

For a standard distance triathlon, we choose to enter the Chester Deva Standard race. By the time it came around, I felt more comfortable swimming. The swim was a 1.5km swim in the River Dee. I was nervous. It was my first time swimming in a river, and I wasn't sure what would happen. Would I be able to swim in a straight line? What if someone kicked me in the face during the mass start? And, most importantly, would the water be as warm as a bath or as cold as a shower when the hot water switches off (which everyone knows is the coldest feeling in the world)?

I shouldn't have worried. I started at the back to avoid the fight for the front. I swam in a straight line, which was brilliant, but, unfortunately, it wasn't always the right line…. and the water was warm. Well, warmish. Well, not cold. Well, okay, it was cold, but I soon adjusted.

The bike race was fantastic, with a trip to Wales, smooth roads, and largely open and traffic-free roads, and the run was a very pleasant three laps around the river, a park and a suspension bridge.

Iain

I wasn't looking at the bridge. I was looking at the supporters hoping to see someone I knew who lived in Chester.

At university, my mate worked for a comedy sketch group. The group comprised three guys and a girl. The girl couldn't act, and she wasn't funny, but she did have large breasts. As talented as the guys were, she was the only one who became a success. She starred in Hollyoaks. The soap is for people who like dramatic over the top storylines - but only if it involves large breasted women and fit guys.

Hollyoaks is set in Chester, but I didn't spot any large breasted women. However, I did see a lot of fit guys... as nearly every person competing was a man.

I was hoping to beat Andrew. I had a secret weapon – I'd ordered a new pair of shorts to go with my new shoes from Bishopbriggs. There was only one problem. They were indecently short: they not only made me look like a knob, but they also showed off my knob.

Unfortunately, I had no alternative pair, so the people of Chester were in for a treat...sorry...a sight. A very horrific sight.

On the morning of the race, registration was next to the hotel where we were staying, so we got up early and headed over. The biggest decision was what swim cap to choose. Our wave had a choice of green/blue. We went for Glasgow Celtic green.

The swim was in the River Dee. The swim was enjoyable. It was 900m approximately up the river before turning and returning. My sighting was good, so I didn't feel I'd zig-zagged too badly.

In the end, I thought the exit was in a different place, so I swam past it and had to turn. Some idiot was following my feet, so he made the same error. When I got out of the water, I turned around and discovered that the idiot was Andrew.

Andrew

Smart.

Iain

A cheat. He'd spotted me at the turning and had decided to have a tow to the finish.

The bike ride was a nice loop out from the city into Wales and back. The road was excellent, and it was virtually car-free.

My aim was to average at least 20mph and stay ahead of Andrew. Luckily, I got out of transition just before him, so I could bomb up the road. Andrew assumed riding at a steady pace would eventually reel me in. It didn't.

I felt good on the run. It must have been my short shorts letting all the air waft about my bits. It was three loops of a riverside course with a water stop on each loop. It was enjoyable, especially once I had worked out Andrew wasn't going to catch me.

At one point, a guy asked what time I was aiming for. I said 48 minutes. He asked if it was okay to pace behind me. I said yes. Unfortunately, he was so close that when a bollard suddenly appeared, I could avoid it, but he collided with it. Sorry.

Other than the shorts, I didn't make any major errors in the race. The longer distance and the scenic course suited me better than the Bishopbriggs race. I have never gone back to race a sprint triathlon since this day.

Now that I'd done a standard triathlon, my next goal was to enter a half Ironman. And then enter a second one so I could claim I'd completed a whole Ironman.

Our first race was Challenge Henley.

Up until 2014, Challenge, a rival company to Ironman, ran a long-distance race in Henley-on-Thames. A place so posh it needs hyphens. The people of Henley hated the triathlon. The closed road race would often be interrupted by a Range Rover or Aston Martin. The locals having decided that 'closed road' only meant closed to riff-raff.

A friend of ours from school had previously completed it and raved about it. That was enough to convince me to do it.

During the bike leg of Challenge Henley, we were cycling towards a feed stop. As we approached, Andrew was behind me. As I braked to collect a water bottle, Andrew continued and touched my back wheel. Suddenly, he flew over the top of his bike onto the feed table before sliding along it into a wall. I stopped and waited for him to get back up. I'm sure this stop cost me a podium place and not the 500 athletes who were faster than me.

Luckily, he was unhurt but a bit shaken. After a quick check that all his bits were still attached to him, he got back on and continued racing.

Andrew

I must admit at this point that Iain was not the only one to notice my tumble. A couple of days later, I was checking a race report thread on a triathlon website when someone commented, "Did anyone see the guy fall headfirst into the feed table?" The only reply was, "Yes. The stupid idiot didn't know how to pick up food on the go."

I didn't know that at the more professional races, where time really matters, the helpers will wait at feed stations and hold out water bottles, energy gels, bars and more. All of which you can snatch as you pass without having to stop. It's great when you know how it works. You can cycle along, stretch out a hand, and someone will just fill it with food. Easy.

I didn't know at the time that this was how the food station worked but, as I was cycling up to it, I saw another rider slow down, reach out a hand and be given a water bottle. I thought I would do the same. I would slow but not stop. I would reach out a hand – what the monkeys, the stupid idiot in front of me has just slammed on the brakes. Dear God, I can't stop. Is that the sky? Or the ground? Why do I hurt all over, and why am I covered in bottles?!

It's clear then: Iain was the stupid idiot who didn't know how to use the feed station, and I was the innocent victim when he braked suddenly to pick up a banana.

Iain

Slightly further up the road, when I experienced a puncture, I shouted at Andrew that I needed to stop and...

Andrew

... I kept going and left him behind. Winners don't stop.

Iain

We enjoyed the race so much we wanted to do it again, but the Henley locals banned triathlons, and the race moved to Weymouth instead.

Weymouth is a place that doesn't need hyphens. If you love ice cream, chips and donkey rides, then this is the town for you. It's also worth a visit if you want to see Leonardo Da Vinci's The Last Supper recreated as a sandcastle.

We drove down on the Friday before the race. We wanted an extra day to get ready before racing on Sunday. Google maps said it would take eight hours from Glasgow, but it didn't consider any other cars or roadworks. It was closer to 12 hours. We should have got a medal for just getting there.

There's plenty of accommodation in the area. We stayed in an ex Ministry Of Defence building that was used to test bombs. This meant the walls were so thick, WiFi and mobile phones didn't work.

Registration took place at a pier, which is the endpoint of the race. The transition areas were about a mile and a half away along the beach. That was okay, but it meant I had to work out where to park our car on race morning. Did I want a long walk to the start but be close to the finish or vice versa?

Registration took a couple of minutes, and we were given all the usual – a race number, a tattoo of the number and different coloured bags to put our transition stuff in. One for the bike, one for the run and one for post-event.

We went back to the hotel to sort everything out. Once we had all the stuff ready, we headed over to transition. At this point, Andrew remembered that he had not put any of his bags into the car. We drove back to the hotel... and then back to transition. As a forfeit, he had to buy me dinner. I picked the expensive options.

The hotel was open for breakfast from 3 am so I popped along at 5 am for some Weetabix. A few others were eating. They all had Weetabix, too, except one man who was having a full English breakfast. I assume he was just a hungry insomniac rather than an athlete.

We choose to park nearer to the finish than the start. As we walked along the beach to transition, we noticed just how fierce the waves were. A quick check of Twitter (always a useful reference to find out what's going on) revealed the waves were so strong the course would be altered, and the full-length race was going to be shortened. Our race would be delayed by 30 minutes.

This meant a long cold wait by the sea as we watched the full distance athletes struggle in the waves. Luckily it calmed down slightly by the time we were due to start. So we decided to give it a go. After all, what's the worst that can happen?

Andrew

I can tell you what happened. You can get rescued by a canoe and learn how hard it is to clean puke from a rubber wetsuit. It was horrific.

The one thing to remember about swimming outdoors is that you need to measure the height of waves in subjective rather than objective terms. While you could say a wave is 30 cm high, the only way to judge the wave is how it compares to your mouth when you swim. Even a small wave will cover your mouth or wash over your head while you try and swim forward. That means every time a wave comes, you need to make sure your mouth is shut; otherwise, you're funnelling the ocean down your gob. And these waves were going to be a big problem as they were choppier than a hyperactive lumberjack.

I'd not swum in the sea since I was on the beach in Coll as a young boy. I just tried to swim as hard as I could over the waves to avoid getting constantly force-fed the English Channel. That was my second mistake. It's easier to swim through a wave or under it than to swim over it. A wave is not a wall. It's better to pierce it than to drive and climb it. But I didn't know that then. So, for the first 1000 metres, I drank more than a bridesmaid on a Hen Night while constantly trying to rise above the waves only to be twisted, turned and ducked down faster than rinsing out a cleaner's mop.

The course was two laps. At the end of the first lap, you ran onto the beach, turned and ran back out again. I didn't make it halfway through that second lap before I was puking with every stroke. Mucus would dribble down my face as one wave hit me, the bile would flow in time with the second wave, and the third would cause it to start again. I could do nothing but turn my head and work on a breath in, stroke, stroke, breath out, spew, repeat strategy.

Until I could take it no more. I called over a support boat and held onto the end of a canoe to try and get some strength back.

"Are you okay?" The canoeist asked.

"I'm okay!" I lied before letting go and trying to swim some more.

It was too late, though. I had nothing left. My retching consisted of nothing but guttural noises deep from my stomach. I had to call the board again.

"I'm done," I said, vomit drying on my swim cap.

A speedboat was called. I was pulled into the back and swiftly brought back to shore.

I didn't feel like I'd lost. On the contrary, it felt like a victory. I had given everything I could, and I could do no more. Or so I thought until, on the shore, someone said: "We'll take your chip, so you won't get an official time, but if you want to keep going, then just go and get changed and grab your bike."

Iain

We had an agreement that we would wait for each other at transition. I had a 10-minute wait for him before he turned up. He said he was delayed as he'd gone for a spin on a boat. I didn't know that was an option.

Experts say you shouldn't change anything before a race. I decided to ignore that advice. I put aero bars on my bike despite the fact I'd never used them before. I didn't have any trouble using them. The experts were wrong.

The race was a 55-mile lap of the local countryside. It was flat with some slight hills. I saw some riders getting off their bikes and walk up the hills. They should move to Scotland and learn what real hills are like.

Highlights of the ride were passing a Tank Museum. The speed signs on the road to it had separate speed limits for tanks and cars.

The strange part of this race was that the run wasn't a standard length of 13.1 miles, but it was 15 miles. Which I thought was a bit unfair, as middle-distance triathlons should finish with a half marathon, not a half and a bit marathon.

We had no choice in the matter, so off we went. The course was two and a half laps of the seafront. There was one section called "the beer mile." Which, unfortunately, did not hand out beers to athletes. Instead, it was pub after pub after pub.

Whilst on the run, we passed a section of beach which contained just one man: a man playing the bagpipes... badly. It was clear why he had that part of the beach to himself. No one else would want to be within earshot.

Even in one of the most southern parts of England, there was still a reminder of home.

The run was good. I felt fit. I left Andrew behind after halfway as his chat was dull. I then made a fatal error. I thought I'd run for a bit with headphones on. I didn't realise doing so was banned.

I've run with headphones during running races. I assumed it was okay during a triathlon race, but it isn't. I discovered that later when I checked my result.

Despite advertising the route as 15 miles. It finished at 12 miles. This was good news for us. But it was bad news for the long course athletes. A screw up in the route meant their race ended short.

After the race, I checked our times and found out Andrew had been DQ'd. It turns out a ride in a boat isn't allowed.

Andrew

I still got a medal, though. Unfortunately, no one asked for my timing chip at the end before handing over the medal for finishing. I should have told them, but then I wouldn't have got a medal, so I didn't. I only mildly regret this.

Iain

And I was marked as DNF, which was news to me. I found out it was due to my headphones.

Andrew

Which sounds unlucky, but I bet it was because he'd run through a checkpoint wearing them. I'd also had mine on, and no one had spotted me because (a) I took them out when running through a checkpoint or food stop; (b) I only used one earbud for a race that ran along the coast and listened on the seaward side while the spectators were on the other side. Smart, but if you follow this advice, then it wasn't me that told you - don't sue me if you get DNF'd

Iain

Despite the DNF, I decided to keep going – we had to take the next step. A long-distance race: Ironman UK.

An Ironman race is a 2.4-mile swim, a 112-mile bicycle ride and then a run of 26.2-mile. The UK race is based in Bolton.

I didn't know much about Bolton other than it was the home of Fred Dibnah, who was famous when I was young for being a steeplejack and television personality. When he died, a statue was erected in his honour. Most people who die in Bolton don't get the honour of a statue when they die. But they might get a mention in a remembrance book at Bolton Wanderer's stadium. It lists all the Bolton fans that died that day. Which is a bit creepy. Does someone have to phone up the hospital and check who the recently deceased supported?

I was scared before the race. I thought to myself, "I could die doing this!"

I have always hoped I would die doing something I love, but I don't love triathlons that much. So instead, I'd prefer to go eating a delicious doughnut. At least then, my last thought would be "yum, what a delicious doughnut" rather than "I wonder if the people of Bolton will build a statue to me or just write my name in the book of remembrance."

It was a valid fear - I'd never cycled more than 100 miles; I'd never swam 3.6 KM, and I certainly hadn't done that and then added a marathon to the end of it. So I got the fear just thinking about it.

To ease my mind, I decided to relax by watching a film at the cinema, but the only thing on was Ant-man. It was terrible. It didn't cheer me up.

We popped into a supermarket after the cinema and got some last-minute snacks. I bought a doughnut. If I'm going to die, then I'll at least have had a doughnut.

I went to bed about 10 pm and set the alarm for 4 am. I slept pitifully and woke early. I could hear the rain pelting against the window. At least that solved the dilemma of what to wear to the start. Instead of clothes, I wore my wet suit.

As I walked to the start, I passed other people in wetsuits, but they were wearing rain smocks over the wet suit! Why??? Surely, they weren't concerned about their wet suit getting wet.

The swim starts with a rolling start. Next, I had to queue in a line. Where I stood in the line represented how quick I thought my swim time would be. I stood at the back.

The swim was two laps of a lake. The rolling start meant there was very little bumping together of athletes at the beginning of the race. It was a surprisingly civilised start, but it was hard to see the yellow buoys marking the course due to the rain.

I did my best, and I was pleased to finish the first lap in 45 minutes. The rain cleared as I started the second lap, but I didn't go any faster. I was still 45 minutes. At least I was consistent. I was surprised when I got out. Andrew was right next to me. I looked at him, he looked at me. "Were you following me?" I asked. "No, you must have been following me!" he replied. Honestly, I didn't see him at all on the course during either lap.

It was a short run from the swim exit to the changing tent. There was only one tent. Men and women had to get changed together. There was a section blocked off at either side if you wanted to get naked. I went there. My plan was to fully dry off and change into bike gear.

The organisers did not do a good job of blocking the view. I could quite clearly see everyone getting changed, and everyone could see me in the buff. I apologise to anyone who got an eyeful. I'd just like to say that the water was very, very cold.

It was still raining when we came out of transition. The first section was a 14-mile urban ride to the start of a two-loop circuit. Each lap had two hills on it. Normally, the hills have huge support out cheering on the riders, but that year, there were only a few hardy souls due to the rain and miserable weather.

I was allowed a special needs bag during the ride. This can contain something you want to eat or drink that the organisers don't provide. Normally athletes use it to put in their own selection of sports gels and drinks.

I used mine to store a Subway sandwich. I wasn't going to spend all day racing without eating some real food. I had to buy the sandwich the day before the race. Unfortunately, the hotel room didn't have a fridge, so instead, I created one using ice cubes and the toilet sink. I was proud of my ingenuity.

The sandwich tasted delicious, but as I was eating it, Andrew approached the special needs stop. He started to slow down, but the man behind him didn't. As a result, the man rode into the back of Andrew. Luckily neither Andrew nor my sandwich were hurt in the accident.

Andrew

Unbelievable. Two feed stops, two accidents and neither was my fault. This time I felt the impact before I saw anything. Again, it was a tumble, a fall, some bottles scattering and then a worrying thought as to whether this was it – was my race over? Was I injured? Or, worse (because at least I can heal), was my bike okay?!

It was, but I don't know how it survived because the bike's time trial bars that hit me were wedged between the back wheel, chain, and seat stays. Thankfully, nothing was bent or broken, except when I tried to get back on, my shoe fell off. The wheel that tightened the laces had snapped off in the fall. My laces were loose, and the shoe wouldn't stay on my foot unless I pressed hard on it when it was attached to the pedal. I was going to have to ride the race almost one-legged and make a passable impression of Long John Silver.

Iain

I made it around the course in a reasonable time. My back was sore, but I was looking forward to running rather than riding a bike.

The rain had stopped, and the sun came out as we left the tent. We had a strategy of running the flat/downhill and walking the uphill. About two minutes after leaving transition, we came to the first hill. It felt strange to stop and walk, but a strategy is a strategy.

The first part of the run took us into Bolton city centre. It was a dull slog along a canal. There were no mile markers. I had to rely on my GPS watch to know how well/badly I was doing.

After this, there were three loops of the city centre. The number of supporters lining the streets was unbelievable. There were people cheering everywhere. At times it was like running into a wall of noise. A wall that liked shouting encouragement. One supporter made me laugh. She shouted "two for the price of one" after spotting myself and Andrew.

The loop was surprisingly hilly. A steady climb out of town and steady descent back. As the hills were long, I abandoned our hill strategy and replaced it with 'the cone game' I'll share this wonderful game so you too can go slightly mental during a race.

It is a very simple game. The course is lined with cones, so pick several cones to run past and then a number to walk between. On the way down the hill on the first lap, we'd do a 4-2 strategy. Four cones running, two cones walking. On the way back up the hill 3-3. The strategy would change depending on how we felt, so if we were tired, we could drop to a 3-cone run, 4-cone walk etc

From this, I learnt Andrew has trouble counting cones. We'd pass one, and he'd say, "was that the second cone or the third?"

After running past so many cones, I now believe I could recognise every cone in Bolton. By the end of the race, I'd assigned them all individual personalities. I might have gone loopy. It was a really good way to get through the run as we could always see where our next run or walk section was.

After many hours of the cone game, we finally crossed the finish line together. We even let one man go ahead of us so that we'd have the carpet clear when we crossed the line. Why cross the finish with a random stranger? They just get in the way of the finish photo! We have a beautiful photo of the two of us walking across the finish together.

As I crossed, a voice announced, "Iain... you are an Ironman!" but all I heard was, "Iain...you did not die!"

Andrew

Iain's covered the race in detail, so I'll just describe it as: swam a bit, rode a bit, ran a bit. Walked a lot. Happy to finish. Will never do it again (or so I thought at the time).

I do, though, want to share six AMAZING tips I learnt from the race that you won't find in the training guide (for good reasons, as will become obvious).

Tip 1: Crash at least once when it's totally not your fault. After riding again after the feedstop crash, I can promise that you'll forget about your legs as you spend the next 20 miles day-dreaming about a bike pump, what you will do with it to the rider who crashed into you and the elaborate torture porn of the Saw films.

Tip 2: Your nose will run. It will never stop. Why not devise your own word for wiping your nose on your sleeve, arm, shoulder, any dry patch of jersey, really? *'Snotting'* anyone? As in, "my nose was runny, so I was snotting on my sleeve to wipe it."

Tip 3: You can leave a special needs bag to pick up during the bike course. You could leave spare gels and energy bars or, you could do as Iain said, and leave a cheese & ham sandwich and a packet of crisps. It may take a couple of minutes to stop and eat it but, after a constant diet of gels, bars and electrolyte drinks, those few minutes were the highlight of my day. Mmmm.... Cheesy Wotsits.

Tip 4: We all run our own races. That's true. But, secretly, in our heart of hearts, we all get a boost when we see a fat bloke struggle. (This is an equal opportunities tip – remember, for the people behind you, you will be their 'fat bloke').

Tip 5: Spectators will cheer you. They'll shout, "You're doing great", "Keep going", "You're running really well",, etc. etc. However, sometimes, you know you're not doing great. You're walking. You're crawling. You've given up and had a cry at the side of the road. At those times, the spectators should shout "You're crap", "You'll never make it", "The fat bloke's beating you". Sometimes we need a bit of humiliation. For your next Ironman, to run faster, why not wear a gimp mask?

Iain

After Ironman UK, I told Andrew I'd never do an Ironman ever again, but I would do Norseman. He asked what Norseman was. I explained all about the ferry and the cold, and the hills.

He said, "I don't fancy that much".

I explained that it is very difficult to get a place at Norseman. They use a ballot system to assign entries. Over 4,000 people apply for 200-ish places. People apply for years without getting in. But if you apply and don't get in, you gain an extra place in the ballot the following year. Therefore, it was worth entering as it would increase the chances of getting in later. If we ever wanted to do it.

Andrew got a place at his first attempt at the draw. My life's dream. Yet Andrew got the place! B*****d!

To warm up for Norseman, we decided to do the Tenby Long Course Weekender, an Ironman distance event but over three days.

Andrew

I've only been to Wales three times (excluding the Deva Triathlon's bike leg in and out).

The first time I'd booked a room in an 18th century inn near Cardiff. It was lovely. Or at least I think it was – I never saw my room. They'd double booked me, and the previous resident hadn't left. They were very apologetic as they were completely sold out. They tried to find me another room, but all they could find was an ex-council house in a room so small it had a sink above the bed to save space. If you want to find out what it's like to brush your teeth while tucked up in bed, then let me know, and I can point you in the direction of "Sheila's B&B".

The second time I was in Wales, I ran down a mountain. I was taking part in the Three Peaks Challenge, and we'd reached Snowdon on hour 21. It took two hours to get to the summit, so we had no choice but to run as fast as we could down the mountain to complete the challenge. I'm not saying I'm a hero for performing such a, well, heroic feat but, if you want to use that term...

The third time I was in Wales, I faced another mountain. I was having dinner and ordered the Eton Mess. The Eton Mountain would have been a better name. It wasn't a plate of food; it was a clear-out of their freezer. A mound of meringue, a field of strawberries and more cream than a cat who's got all the cream. I didn't need a sink above my bed that night; I had no teeth left after that sugar.

But, in all the times I've been to Wales, I've never realised how long it takes to drive through it. It's around 130 miles from Chester to Tenby on the south coast, but four hours later, you'll still be driving through a series of road signs that look like my texts before auto-correct fixes them. Wales is a long way away.

The Long Course weekend does what it says on the tin. It's a weekend where you can participate in a long course triathlon (Ironman Wales) but over three days rather than one. It also offers shorter distances each day.

We were due to take part in the 2.4-mile swim on Friday, the 112-mile ride on Saturday and the marathon (for Iain) and the half marathon (for me, as I didn't want to run 26 miles a few weeks before Norseman) on the Sunday. But things didn't quite go to plan as not only is Wales a long way away, it's also quite hilly...

Iain

I enjoy watching channel four program 'Grand Designs'. One episode featured property in Tenby. A lifeboat station that had been converted to a house.

I was very excited when I realised the swim course had passed by the house. I imagined the presenter of the show Kevin McCloud standing at the house. He would look out, spot my swim, and utter his catchphrase, "I admire your ambition!"

It was a beautiful summer's evening for the swim. The sea was calm, and 2000 people had gathered on the beach to attempt the race.

I was feeling confident I'd beat Andrew. His last experience at Weymouth has made him hate swimming in the sea. I love swimming in the sea - the choppier the waves, the better!

The race started with an impressive firework display, and then 2,000 folk ran towards the water. The sighting was easy in good conditions. Aim for the cliffs, then turn right and aim for Kevin McCloud, before turning right again and aiming for the beach.

Andrew

Which would be easy as there was no water, which was a problem when you're swimming.

We were one hour from starting, and the tide was out. We could jog to the first buoy and walk half the course. However, as the beach was flat, it didn't take long for the water to rise, and I took off my trainers and put on my goggles.

By the time we started, as fireworks exploded, blanketing the start in smoke, we actually had some water to swim in, which was good, as there were 2000 people behind us in wetsuits.

The start area was crowded. Somehow, we ended up near the front of the pack. The swimmers weren't separated into different groups, so it was everyone for themselves as we were herded into a big pen on the beach. It was good to be near the start because even with only a few hundred around us, the water was crowded for the first 10 minutes. Everyone was turning, kicking and trying to find their rhythm. 2,000 people mean 4,000 legs and 4,000 elbows to avoid.

But the swimmers quickly became spread out. The swim course at the Long Course Weekend takes in two laps of Tenby harbour in a rough anti-clockwise triangle along the coast, back through some fishing boats, before turning back to shore for an Australian exit, which is not an upside-down exit, but a short run along the beach before returning to the start for a second lap. I don't know why it's called an Australian exit. It should be an Austrian exit as you're surrounded by land.

I finished five minutes behind Iain. The second lap felt easier than the first. However, at one point, I spotted one man clutching the anchor rope of a fishing boat with an expression that said, "I will only release this for death or a rescue boat – and I will gladly accept death than swim another meter!"

I was nervous about the swim. Since being rescued at Weymouth, I hadn't swum in the sea, and I knew I needed this swim as good preparation for Norseman. I needed to know I could swim the distance and that I could swim in the sea.

So, while I was feeling tired towards the end of the swim, I was also happy as I knew the distance was okay, and I'd overcome my nervousness about swimming in the sea.

Iain

I once watched a programme about people who swim on the English Channel. The pilot of a boat told one swimmer: "You need to be prepared."

The swimmer replied, "prepared for what?"

He was told: "After doing this, you'll never be the same again."

Which implied some life-changing profoundness will be gained through completing the challenge, but I've found that's not always the case. At university, I challenged a friend to eat 12 Cadbury creme eggs in one sitting. I told him: "After doing this, you'll never be the same again". I was right. He was never the same again. He used to love creme eggs but now can't abide anything with caramel in it.

I don't think I've learnt anything profound by completing a race, but I have learnt one simple lesson. I don't like racing in the cold, rain, and wind.

I wish I could tell you how I overcame the hellish weather on the bike course the next day, but I can't. It was wet and miserable, so I did one lap of the course. That was more than enough.

Andrew

On the next and final day, to start the run, a samba band played as we walked from Pembroke Castle in a parade to the start line at the end of the High Street. However, to start the bike leg, we went to a car park, and a man in a fluorescent tabard said, "You might as well go then". I think the bike leg needs to get its act together.

The start of the half-marathon was impressive. Arguably, more impressive than the marathon we'd watched start two hours earlier in Tenby.

The marathon runners start in the centre of Tenby, run to Pembroke and then come back via the half marathon route. The start is crowded with a couple of narrow 90-degree turns. The half marathon starts on a wide street, the main street of Pembroke, and has music, a parade, and something Tenby can't top – a huge castle.

Also, Pembroke has Constance Brown's Cafe/chippy. We'd discovered it on Friday when we popped over to see the castle. Constance opened the cafe in 1928 and was still serving chips there over 80 years later at 102 years old. She'd died at 104, but the cafe hadn't changed. Neither had the prices, which was handy when we were looking for a cheap and quick lunch.

Originally, I would have run the marathon, but that was before I was successful in the Norseman ballot. Now, with four weeks to go, it would be stupid to try and run a marathon and then race Norseman a month later. It was the right choice as, while the first few miles were flat, the next 10 were more up and down than a nodding dog.

I'd decided to keep a steady pace, Iain decided to run. Within a mile, he was gone. I didn't want to try and keep up; I had a plan, and I stuck to it. I listened to Hamilton, the musical, and kept a steady pace. A pace which would, I soon find out, overtake Iain.

At mile 10, I saw him. I felt strong, so I poked him in the back then ran away. He didn't follow, and I had a clear lead for the last three miles, largely downhill until a vicious wee hill half a mile from the finish.

And then – a cock-up.

There was a red-carpet finish. I thought the start of the carpet was the finish line as it was marked with a gantry. I sprinted. I crossed the line. I stopped. I got told off by a man in the crowd who said, "You're not finished yet – it's another 20 metres."

Iain

Thankfully the weather was a lot better on Sunday. I had beaten Andrew in the swim but lost him on the bike leg, so the run was the decider. I was confident of victory, having beaten him in most running races over the last few years. I was too confident.

I started off way too fast and bonked at mile 9. I thought I'd done enough to stay ahead of him, but I was wrong. He caught and passed me. I didn't see it again until the end. He was the deserved winner... this time.

Andrew

Next stop, Norseman.

CHAPTER NINE: NORSEMAN

Iain

In the run-up to Norseman, I was reminded of when the gym manager of the Western Isles Leisure Centre said to Andrew and me: "If you two brothers were clever, you'd only have one gym membership". Little did he know that's what we were already doing. The membership was a photo ID, so, as we are identical twins, we would pass the card between us to whichever one of us wanted to use it.

Similarly, we can both use each other's bikes. We have a mountain bike, a time trial bike, an aero bike, a cyclocross bike, a road bike with a 28 gear cassette and a road bike with a 32 gear cassette. A 32 gear cassette is helpful for a hilly course as it makes climbing them easier.

For Norseman, Andrew decided to use my 32 gear cassette bike.

This decision had one problem. We only had one bike bag, and it was at Andrew's house. He would have to get it from his loft to my house to pack up the bike for the race.

The day before we were due to fly, he called to say he had the bag. Could he drop it off the next day? He then added, "There's just one problem. I've injured myself lifting it down from the loft!"

Idiot. He'd trained for seven months without injury, and now he'd hurt himself getting the bike bag. The race was nearly over before it began. Although it did make me think this may be karma coming back — revenge for getting a place and stealing my dream.

Andrew went to a physio. The physio worked wonders, and Andrew was patched back together before the flight. He was as good as new, although he was 38 at the time, so the phrase should be – as good as new-ish. The physio wasn't a miracle worker.

We flew in the evening from Edinburgh to Oslo. It's a short flight, but we landed after midnight due to the time difference, which in Norway is just as bright as midday in the UK, except you can hear people snoring.

Once we landed, it was another hour to retrieve the bags. We then headed outside to collect a taxi. The driver took one look at the bike bag and said it would not fit in his car, and even if it did, there wouldn't be room for the two of us.

I proved him wrong. I managed to squeeze the bike in the boot, and I managed to sit in the back. The driver mumbled something which sounded like a protest and then bumped the fare up to twice the standard rate. Welcome to Norway.

The following day, we went to breakfast. The hotel has a waffle machine. A hot burning griddle was lying open on a table. If British health and safety were here, they'd go mad. Thankfully they were not, so I threw caution to the wind and made a waffle while risking severe injury. Thankfully, I escaped with just minor burns, but it was worth it for a delicious waffle.

We also took the opportunity to cut bread and steal the cheese and ham. I always make lunch from whatever is available at a hotel's breakfast bar, which is okay when a hotel provides a cheese and ham buffet but not so good when I have a cornflake sandwich.

According to our car rental instructions, our hotel was across the road from the car rental location. We headed across the street. It wasn't the car rental location. Even though that was what was written on our booking, they told us we had to go back to the airport. Oh well, we had plenty of time; it was only 300km to Eidfjord (our next hotel stop). That won't take long. We can afford the delay.

An hour later than intended, we're on our way. The car was big and brand new. The man at the rental desk tried to sell us a GPS. We said no. When we got to the car, it had a GPS built into it. I'm glad we didn't pay for a second one.

We entered the destination into the GPS as Eidfjord. The GPS thought for a minute and then told us it'll take five hours. Nonsense. It's not that far. The time must be wrong. I was right. It was wrong. It took longer.

Driving in Norway is slow. Cars don't go above 50 mph, and even rarer do they overtake. This may partly be due to their being barely a straight road between Oslo and Eidfjord. It may also be due to speed limits that I unintentionally broke throughout the journey. I wish I could tell you the scenery was stunning, but it required total concentration to ensure I didn't miss the next turn on the road. Andrew, on the other hand, raved about the view. I felt like Morgan Freeman in Driving Miss Daisy - if Miss Daisy was a lazy triathlete who claimed he couldn't drive because he needed a rest in the car to better prepare for his race.

Eidfjord was a beautiful small town. Mountains surrounded it, and it was the perfect setting for a race. Unfortunately, we couldn't stay in town as there was limited accommodation, so I booked the closest place. A hotel nearby that was quirky but nice. When we arrived, a fellow competitor was arguing with the owner about the price of the room. He couldn't understand why he was asked to pay more for his twin room due to six people. He argued that he should pay for two. I admired his logic, but the owner insisted he paid for the number of people sleeping in the room and not by the number of beds.

We left them arguing and decided to visit the biggest waterfall in Norway. It was a few miles away, so it was back into the car. There was a lot of driving on this trip. Norseman should be called DrivingMan.

We parked near the viewpoint of the falls. It was a great view and well worth a visit. Although the markers showing where people had died did make me extra careful with my footing.

We headed back to Eidfjord to get some supplies and to check out the town. I decided to test the water temperature in the only manner I knew how. I stuck my hand in the fjord. It wasn't too cold. No different from Scottish conditions.

We took some photos of the town, and then we headed back to our accommodation to get some sleep. Breakfast was supposed to be waffles. Yay. Unfortunately, they'd all been eaten. The buffet had opened at 8 am, and everything was eaten by 8:01 am. Triathletes like to eat, and they want to get up early.

The waitress said she'd never seen so many folk turn up at once. And then wondered how they all slept in the same room. I said, "stacked like pancakes".

Looking at the 'competition', it was clear there were some very fit athletes present, and they were just the supporters of the real athletes. I did wonder what they made of Andrew and me. I didn't ask. I didn't want to hear what a Norwegian sounds like laughing.

We headed into town to register and to get the bike serviced. The flight over had damaged one of the disc brakes. It was slightly bent. I wasn't worried. The worst-case scenario was that we would have to bash it with a hammer.

Andrew

I was worried. I was ready to blame Iain as I'm pretty sure the bike was bashed when he squeezed it into the taxi back at the airport.

Iain

Whilst the bike got serviced, we went for a swim.

HUUB clothing company had sponsored a practice session. Many athletes took the opportunity to have a go at swimming the final section of the swim route. Andrew immediately noticed a problem. He'd forgotten his swim goggles. Idiot (again!)

He went to the HUUB clothes stall (conveniently set up next to the swim) to buy a new pair. They were 450 Norwegian Krona which, when converted to British Pounds, came to f***ing expensive.

Andrew

I paid up. It was a stupid (and expensive) mistake.

Iain

The swim was great. The water was chilly but not too bad. I overheard a man from Dubai complain about how cold it was. I think his and my idea of hot and cold differ wildly.

Andrew

I was lucky enough to swim in the Arabian Sea a couple of years ago. I had a stopover in Dubai, the hotel was next to the beach, and I decided that a 42-degree day would be an ideal time to swim in the ocean. I was wrong. As soon as I got in, I felt like a teabag in a cup of lukewarm tea. The water was too hot. It would have made a pleasant temperature for soup. Every time I ducked my head, I felt like I would come out as red as a lobster after five minutes in the pot.

What was going on? I'd never swum in water like that before. There was no cold shock when I started to wade in. No head chill from ducking below a wave. It was almost... pleasant. I couldn't take it. It was just too nice.

So, whilst I had braced myself for near arctic chills and icy waters. It was pretty warm for Scottish swimmers. The fjord was 16 degrees, so we jumped in without wetsuits.

"Are you mad?' A man cried.

"No, we're Scottish," we said.

"No, you must be SALMON!" He said firmly as he finished pulling on gloves, socks and three swim caps.

And that made me realise that everyone's idea of extreme is different. For him, 16 degrees was as cold as a Penguin eating a Magnum ice cream in the middle of the Arctic circle. Whilst, for us, 16 degrees was as comfy as a towel straight from the tumble dryer.

But swimming in warm water is just madness. The whole point of swimming is to cool off, to feel nice and refreshed, and you just can't do that with an ocean warm enough to make Earl Grey tea.

That's why I doff my swim cap to all the warm weather swimmers. The swimmers who can swim all year round and never reach that optimum temperature of 14 degrees when the water is as refreshing as a gazpacho soup. The one's who never get the benefit of swimming with a five-inch-thick wetsuit so buoyant it could turn you into the balloon. After swimming in the Arabian Sea, I declare that all who swim in warm water are truly the extreme swimmers.

Iain

The first thing I noticed about the swim was that the water wasn't very salty, which must be due to water flowing off the mountains.

Andrew did one lap of the course. I did two. The swim reassured him that the big one wouldn't be too bad. All was well. The bike serviceman had finished with the bike, and it now worked like a charm. Things were looking up until later that day....

"Feck, feck, feck, feck!" I thought to myself.

The bike was making a sound. Not a good sound like wiii-iiissshhhh of speed but a grrrnnnnnhhhkkk of metal. It seemed to be coming from the front wheel.

Earlier, I'd noticed a big climb behind our hotel and thought it would be a good test for the bike, but on the way down, the wheel had started crunching.

I stopped and spun the wheel. It was sticking. This was a major problem. Norseman is hard enough without doing it on a bike that seemed to have the brakes permanently on.

I headed down from the climb and hoped I could look at the issue without Andrew finding out. I didn't want to worry him.

Annoyingly he was standing outside our accommodation as I rolled in. I had to tell him about the problem. He was worried. The bike service was now shut, and the race was tomorrow. "We need a plan," he said

"We need Google," I replied.

I started googling "grinding disc brake pads".

Andrew looked worried. He repeated, "we need a plan."

I told him to get the bike

"No, we need a plan."

"Get the bike!"

"We need a plan."

What's the point of a plan if we don't have the bike? He didn't seem to grasp that the first step would always be to get the bike, whatever the plan was.

He stropped off to get it.

Andrew

Do you pick up a recipe book before reaching into the bag for a handful of King Edward Potatoes? No. Nor do you pick up a spoon before you know what you're going to cook. Getting the bike was pointless without a plan. I didn't stop.

Iain

I found the video I wanted. It explained how to loosen the callipers on the brake.

Andrew

And while I was away, he did what I said and worked out a plan. I was right.

Iain

He came back. I took out an Allen key and loosened the callipers. The wheel ran smooth. Andrew looked relieved - and worried. He may have secretly hoped that this would get him out of having to race.

We celebrated our achievement by having Norwegian meatballs. There's a reason I'd never heard of them over their more famous Swedish rivals. They tasted disgusting.

Andrew

If a murderer could choose a last meal before his execution, then they would select lobster or steak or a burger made from the juiciest cow in the world. If the victim's family could choose a meal as revenge, they would 100% choose Norwegian meatballs.

Iain

Race day. If 3 am is an ungodly time, getting up at 2.30 am is even worse.

Today was the day. It was now or never, which is a strange expression. It should be "It was now or never or...in a minute! Can't you see I'm busy? I'll get to it when I can!"

We left the B&B and headed to Eidfjord. There was plenty of parking spaces near the ferry, but Andrew refused to use them. He was worried that the police would turn up and find us. It's

3 am. I think the police had better things to do than check anyone is parking illegally.

Andrew

As a lawyer, I know that the law applies 24 hours a day. You don't get a break just cause the policemen are asleep. Though now I think about it, Iain's attitude would explain why so many burglaries happen at night.

Iain

We parked at the local school. On the walk to the ferry, I pointed out to Andrew all the cars parked in the spaces he had said not to use.

The port was busy. A lot of athletes and supporters were there. I looked at the ferry and noticed it had a TV lounge. And comfy chairs. And it was showing the Olympics. Extreme Triathlon? My Arse.

On the way into transition, Andrew had to show that his bike's front and backlights work and that he had a reflective jacket.

A volunteer checked his jacket and said it was not reflective enough. It was very yellow, but it was not reflective. Andrew blamed it on buying a cheap one from Decathlon. Idiot.

Luckily the volunteer had a spare jacket that he gave to Andrew. The race winner gets a black T-shirt, but I bet Andrew is the only competitor who has a Norseman branded reflective vest. I wished Andrew luck, and he headed onto the ferry.

Andrew

I took the bike and bag, and I joined the queue to board the ferry. I needed to be on board by 4 am and, through the windows, I could see the Olympic opening ceremony playing on a TV in a lounge. I remember that it's not quite a morning, that it's still Friday night no matter what time my watch shows.

The deck of the boat was empty as everyone was sitting in

lounges upstairs. I sat beside a Canadian and a Swedish man who had the same type of wetsuit as me. "You must have had the shortest journey?" I say to him to make conversation. "I drove for 14 hours," he said.

At 4:45 am, I apply Vaseline to my neck and ask the Canadian to zip up my wetsuit. I wished both luck, and I went down to the car deck, which was filling up with athletes getting ready for the race to start.

At the back of the deck, I saw a hose pumping and spraying seawater. I knew I needed to adjust to the cold water, so I walked straight into it –

– and start hypeventilating –

– so I ducked out of the spray, then ducked in again.

And again. And again. For 10 minutes. Until the water no longer felt cold, I could breathe normally until I felt ready to jump.

A tannoy announced the jump would start in two minutes. I put on my large swim cap to cover my ears, my goggles and my race cap. I walked as close to the front as I could. I didn't want to wait. I wanted to go straight in without hesitation.

The jump starts.

People fall like lemmings in front of me. It only takes a few seconds for me to stand on the edge of the deck. Another second for me to jump. To raise my hand to my googles to make sure they stay in place. Then I struck the water, and it's cold and dark, and surrounding me, holding me tight in its grip, but it's not too cold. And as I kick to push myself up and break the surface, I see lights on the coastal road, dawnlight peaking over the fjord, and I grin. And I shout in joy. I'd faced my fear, and I'd won.

There was a line of canoes ahead of me. I swam over, using breaststroke and a few crawl strokes to acclimatise more to the water.

I looked back, and people were still falling. The boat squats on the water, and I know that everything will be okay.

I floated for a few minutes. "Enjoy this," I told myself. Dark cliffs tower above, in front and to the side. The water is cool. And fresh, the winter snows create a freshwater layer that masks the salt. The canoes drift. I stay near the front, floating between two canoes. I know everyone will pass me, but I like the thought of being in the lead, if only for a second.

I wait for the ferry's horn to sound.

RRRRRRRRRRRRRRRRRR-
WWWWWWWWWWWWWWWWWWWWWUUUUUURR
RRPPPP

And we're off. I'm quickly overtaken, but I settle into a rhythm. 1 – 2 – 3 – 4. 1 – 2 – 3 – 4. And I breathe to my left every time I count four.

I have no idea where I was. I can see lights in the fjord ahead. Daylight awakens, and I know which direction to go, but I can't tell how far I'd gone or how far I had to go.

Even when I turn the corner of the fjord and face Eidfjord directly, I don't know if this is one mile or one metre away.

At times, I followed the feet of a swimmer in front. At others, I have a Siamese twin. A swimmer is breathing to my right, keeping pace and only a foot away. Sometimes I even swim near a pack, though I'm on my own most of the time. I'm further out than others, but I don't try and move closer as I'm heading in the right direction.

In Eidfjord, they light a bonfire on a beach to help you find your way. I didn't know this when I swam, but I could see an orange light, and I used that to get me to the first (and only) bouy. From there, it's about 500 metres across Eidfyord pier to a small rocky beach. This final stretch is brutal. It was the same area we'd swum in a practice session. Yesterday, however, it was flat calm. Today, the wind had picked up waves, and the current was against me. But I was nearly 'home'. I kept going.

I thought there were another 100 metres to the finish around the pier, but I was wrong; it was only 20 metres. I kicked my legs to try and get some feeling into them. I wobbled on the stony ground when I stood up. I tried to balance and looked at the people on the beach and the pier above to see if I could find Iain.

I started to jog. (As if it would help). I was happy. I was done. I told myself: "You will never do this again!" the same thing I told myself at IronMan UK. I'm good at lying to myself.

Iain

I decided to drive down the coast to watch the start. Surprisingly no one else had thought of this, so I was on my own watching the start. I can't imagine what people did in town. It must have been boring waiting for the swimmers to come back.

After they jumped in, I headed back to town. I stopped at a pier near the yellow buoy and watched the race leaders zoom past. My watch said 50 minutes, so it seemed like they were slow, or the race had started late. I later found out the swim times were slow due to a strong tide.

I got back to the pier in enough time to watch Andrew come out. I showed him over to the transition point and helped him get changed. About half the swimmers were still in the water, so his swim time was pretty good.

I sent him off and said I'd see him in a couple of hours at the top of the hill.

I noticed a man at the pier had made fresh pancakes. I buy four so that Andrew will have a treat at the top of the hill. I then eat two. Two would still be a treat. He need never know there was four.

Andrew

WTF! There was four!

Iain

I then headed back to the hotel to get some breakfast. Mmm… waffles. It was a hard life being a support team. I packed up our stuff and left the accommodation.

I then lost Andrew. I'm sure I saw him a minute previously. I passed him in my car. I gave him a wave, and then I parked at the next available parking spot. I waited 20 minutes, and he did not go past. I was high above Eidfjord, on a plateau. Due to thick mist, visibility is 100m, and it's cold. I wouldn't like to be in a car in these conditions, let alone on a bike.

I decided something had gone wrong. He's gone past, and I didn't notice, or something's happened before he got here. I decided to head back down the road. I drove for 10 minutes, but I didn't spot him. It's now colder and wetter than it was. I imagine he will be wondering where I've gone.

I raced along the road. After another 10 minutes of driving, I still had not spotted him. After another 20 minutes, I'm worried. Something must have gone wrong. I continue driving until I finally spot a very cold and wet looking cyclist ahead. It was Andrew.

Andrew

The bike leg of Norseman is 112 miles inland from the pier at Eidfjord to the town of Austbygde. It starts with a 1,250m climb to Dyranut, a long stretch along a high plateau, descends back down before the second half hits you with four increasingly longer and harder hills before a 15-mile descent to the second transition.

The weather forecast all week had been for a north-westerly tailwind and for conditions to be mostly dry. That changed on Friday night. It was going to rain for most of the morning and afternoon. I'd brought waterproof cycling shorts, shoes and a jacket with me, so I wore those straight from transition, even though it was dry when I changed. I thought it would be enough. I was wrong.

The bike leg starts with a few miles along a flat road from Eidfjord before the climbing starts. The cliff face rises on either side, we follow the old road around the edge of the rock face, dart through tunnels lit by candles, and it feels like we've travelled back in time. We've left the modern world behind. The road is pitted, with potholes easy to avoid; the drops are steep and tumble down like the waterfalls that scour the sides. I settle into an easy rhythm in my lowest gear and essentially keep pace with the riders around me. Occasionally, I overtake riders on TT bikes standing on the pedals while I sit down and pass them on the left.

The views are stunning. Wisps of clouds hug the tops of cliff-like triumphant climbers about to summit, looking down I can see glimpses of other riders, brightly coloured ants against the dark grey cliff roads, and I keep repeating in my head:

"Enjoy this."

Because what else is there to do? If I cannot look round and feel that this is the only place I want to be today, that these sights are glimpses of landscape that I'm privileged to see and be part of it, then I don't deserve to do this.

"Enjoy this."

The climb consists of two distinct sections. The first strikes through the mountain, climbing through a cleft in the rock like the remnants of a giant's axe strike; the second is a long climb towards the summit, through moorland and patches of snow along the sides of the road. It's in the second section that it starts to rain. And rain.

I don't mind the rain at first. I'm prepared; I have my waterproofs, and I've used them before in bad conditions, so I know they'll be okay. But then the clouds lower. Visibility drops, and now it's not only raining; I can only see 50 – 100 metres at a time. This is why we need to wear a high-viz vest and use lights for the whole route. I'm grateful for them. Not for me, but to see others, that I'm not alone.

The next few hours are an increasing struggle. The climb goes further than the profile suggests. Long shallow climbs where, even with a tailwind, progress is slower than I'd hoped. TT bike shoot by. I can't keep up, nor do I try. I went for a climbing bike and comfort, not speed.

Spots that I remembered from driving across the plateau are rendered indistinct by the clouds. A lake with two black houses on the shore. Three turf houses at the side of the road. It's always too late when I spot them. But still, I tell myself to smile. I'm happy. But wet.

The support cars can't join you on the climb; I saw them in a traffic jam going down the mountain as I climbed up; the single road means there's no place to stop. I've brought enough food for two and half hours, eating every thirty minutes — my standard 'meals' of bars and gels. But after two and half hours, I'd yet to see Iain.

I thought I saw him at one point. A black Hyundai estate with 91 – my number – on a sticker on the back. He was down a short lane and trying to reverse the car. I'd passed him before I could stop. I thought if it was him, that he was reversing because he'd seen me and was going to follow. I was wrong.

It was another hour before I saw him. Every time a car passed, I would hope it was him. After 30 minutes, I started to worry. I wondered if he'd had a puncture or, worse, an accident. Every black car that passed was met with a searching look of its back window. 201. 15. 134. Not 91.

I was relieved when I finally saw him. I was soaked through, and I had run out of food. He pulled in a couple of hundred metres ahead of me. "I've got you a pancake," he said.

Iain

Is one pancake a treat? (I might have eaten the second while waiting at the top of the plateau and before I realised I missed him).

Andrew

By this point, I'd been thinking of quitting. I was starting to shake with hypothermia. I was losing the feeling in my hands. The rain was bouncing off the road, and I wasn't sure if I could carry on for another five hours like this.

"Put this on," Iain said as I stripped off my hi-viz jersey, waterproof jacket and cycling jersey while sheltering under the open boot of the car.

He gave me a new base layer, my thicker cycling jersey, a fleece, a Goretex jacket and full-length waterproof trousers. I thought he wanted to keep warm whilst we were stopped. I didn't realise that I was going to wear this for the next 60 miles.

"I'll go to the next town," I said. The warm clothes had done their job in persuading me to carry on.

"Just keep this on," Iain said. And I did. I got back on my bike and pedalled off, wearing more gear than I would if I was climbing a mountain.

But it worked. I warmed up. I stopped shaking. The weather was still awful, but as I descended in Grillo, it became warmer as I left the plateau.

In town, I met Iain again. "I'll get to the end," I said while thinking ", Enjoy this, you won't be doing it again."

Iain

It turns out he had cycled past me. My parking spot was in an awkward place. He assumed it wasn't my car. I must have missed him as I was too busy concentrating on not crashing the car as I reversed into the space.

I thought he would be angry, so I pulled out my trump card – the pancake.

I thought quickly and then asked him.

"Do you want a Twix too?"

I offered him the sweet. He was cold, and his hands were shaking, but at least he had a chocolate biscuit snack.

He said he was struggling to bike due to the cold. The weather was terrible, and it did not look likely to improve.

I had some Goretex trousers with me, a thick fleece top and a jacket. He took off his wet clothes and replaced them with new ones. He now looked ready to climb Everest.

At least he was dry and warm, even if he was not very aerodynamic.

He said he would cycle to the next town before deciding whether to carry on. I hoped he would keep going. It would have been a shame to finish at that point.

We passed the next town and came off the plateau. This section was supposed to be faster and more downhill than the first part of the course. Thankfully he was feeling warmer and decided to continue.

The next half of the race has four climbs. They are all manageable climbs. We have a rhythm for the next 50 miles where I would drive a short distance up the road. He would then either bike past me or pull in to get some food. It seemed to work well. As the bike route now was short, manageable sections.

At the top of the last climb, I had to stop supporting him. It was all downhill from there, so I left him to it and headed to the second transition. There were only a few people there. Most of the competitors had already been through. I went for a walk and discovered nearby a couple posing for wedding photos.

Andrew eventually arrived.

Andrew

The second half of the course was a lot different to the first. It's felt more part of civilisation, and you can see towns, wider roads, and more road signs for evidence of other people.

There are four climbs in this section, nothing too challenging or too long but each steady. The final climb is the longest, taking you up to and across a dam. It's here that a Norwegian woman stood on the porch of a remote house and shouted: "Well done, Andrew, keep going!". It took me a few minutes to figure out she must be following a Norseman tracker on the official website, which shows every competitor's location. It's also here where the support of other teams becomes invaluable. I was going the same pace as a few other riders, so I not only passed Iain every 40 minutes or so, I also passed other support crews who shouted encouragement.

By now, I've decided I'd finish at T2. My temperature was screwy, I'm not sure whether I should be running after hypothermia, and the final climb on the run course is looking increasingly beyond me. I decide to be sensible and finish while I have Iain as support.

The final descent for 15 miles, through thick forest, small villages of colourful chalet houses, and, even better, it's also the first time it's dry. The sun peeks out, though not for long, and I'm hitting 35 miles an hour on the sharp descent and 25 mph on the flats. It's too fast, too late, though. I'm still dressed like Ranulph Fiennes.

At the second transition, I tell the timekeeper that I'm done. There is not a single doubt in my head that I'm doing the right thing. After 112 miles, my legs feel okay. I still feel strong(ish), but the desire to keep going has been washed out by the cold and the rain. The thought of running thought that again is more than I take. I'm done. But I loved it. Every cold, wet, miserable minute of it.

Iain

"How're the legs?" I asked.

"Sore," replied Andrew.

He was lying in bed in Rjukan. A tiny town at the base of "Zombie Hill." The famed section of Norseman where runners switch from running on the flat to climbing Mt. Gaustatoppen.

I felt fit, so I decided to take the bike out and head up the mountain. The climb was challenging, but it's more a mental thing than anything else. It doesn't have many hairpins. Each section felt like a long slog.

On the road, people had painted zombies or inspirational words. It was easy to tell the UK supporters as they've painted slogans on the wrong side of the road.

I stopped once I got to the Funicular railway that takes tourists to the top of the mountain. I noticed it was open, so I headed back down, hoping to the hotel. I convinced Andrew that we should go to the top. It felt like the logical conclusion to our trip should be on top of the mountain.

Thankfully he was up for it, and even more, thankfully, he had also packed up all our stuff.

The funicular was great. It was split into two trains. One that took us into the mountain and then another that took us to the top. From that top, it was just a few hundred metres to the Norseman hut. The famed end of the race. It was great to see the finish line, even if it was 24 hours later.

We took some pictures and recorded a video of Andrew crossing the finish line.

We then popped into the hut to buy waffles. All races should have waffles at the finish. They might not make good meatballs, but Norway sure knows how to make a waffle.

On the way back down, an older couple was sitting in our train carriage. The man said to his wife, "not much to see, was there?"

Not really. It was very cloudy on top, but if we hadn't gone up, we would have regretted it.

The aim of the trip was to enjoy a Norseman adventure. We had an adventure, and we enjoyed it. What more to life is there than that?

Andrew

Waffles?

Iain

Good point. Later that year, I applied again for Norseman. I didn't get in, so I applied for another famous race - Escape From Alcatraz. It also has a ballot entry system. I didn't get into that either. But can you guess who did?

Andrew

I did. I should play the lottery.

Iain

As I didn't get into either of those races, I instead decided to enter a local race - Ironman Edinburgh 70.3

When the race was announced, the start was Gosford House – one of Scotland's grandest homes. I had always wanted to visit it, so I was disappointed when the start was subsequently moved to a nearby town. Instead of racking my bike in a beautiful estate, I racked my bike in a field next to a Lidl supermarket.

Once Andrew and I had racked our bikes, we to get some food - nachos and ice cream. Separately. Not together. That would taste awful.

The next day we were the last ones into the water as queuing for a toilet had taken priority over queuing to get into the water. Maybe the pre-race meal was not a good choice. We should stick to pasta.

The swim was shortened due to bad weather. I could see Andrew was nervous.

Andrew

"Is it safe?"

In the film Marathon Man this quote is repeated as Sir Laurence Olivier performs an increasingly painful dental treatment on Dustin Hoffman.

In Ironman Edinburgh, this quote is repeated by everyone on the start line as we gaze out to sea.

"Is it safe?"

The week before the race, we recce the course to check the swim start and cycle part of the bike route. It was windy, over 20 mph, and the water at Preston Links at Prestonpans was choppy and covered in white caps. A woman got out of a car beside us. She was wearing an Ironman hoodie and an Ironman cap. So was her father, who came out next. "Are you racing?" We said, which was a daft question as he was clearly in his seventies... luckily, she answered for him. She was racing. And she was there to practice the swim. But, on looking at the water, she said: "Not today. I'm not going out in that!"

She had an English accent, so we thought she wasn't local (though, with Edinburgh so close, an English accent could be local), and we tried to reassure her: "It won't be like this next week – this is a one-off. It's just a bit of wind."

Unfortunately for her, we were utterly wrong. It wasn't just a bit of wind. It was the start of a week-long howl that kept going all through Monday to Friday, sped up on Saturday and wasn't due to slow down until the race was over.

On Saturday, the forecast was for winds of 15mph plus. Too strong for a calm swim. By Saturday night, the organisers were predicting a shortened swim and by 6 am, they'd shortened it from 1900m to 950m. One lap of a course that had been re-arranged to try and avoid the worst of the currents.

But not at the start. The first 100 metres would be straight into the waves and current and wind — the perfect storm.

For the first 100 metres, I could see people struggling. Not only was there the shock of cold water, the tightness of my chest constricting, the shallow breaths and the constant gulps of salt water as I tried to time the waves correctly so that my mouth is, and this is the crucial bit, above the waves, not below them. But there was also the need to sight the first buoy, to avoid fellow athletes and to generally survive in conditions that even blockbuster movie shark Jaws would say: "Don't go into the water!".

But, after the first turn, as we swam along the beach, not out to sea, the conditions improved. It was easier to breathe with the waves at my side than right in front.

Of course, being an idiot, I then decided I had to clear my goggles as they'd filled with condensation. I tried to duck under the water, remove my goggles to rinse them out, then put them back on in one smooth fluid motion.

It didn't happen.

I ducked. I spluttered. I got salt in my eyes. I couldn't see. I swallowed half of the Firth of Forth, I ended up swimming in the wrong direction – but I did all that in one smooth fluid motion, so at least I got something right.

For the rest of the swim, I had leaky goggles, and I had to keep taking them off to clear them of water. While when they were on, I had to keep one shut to avoid the salt water seeping in. And swimming with one eye is not easy – just ask Captain Hook, if he'd had two eyes, he'd have been able to swim away from that crocodile.

Despite my one eye, I got to the final buoy and turned back to shore. The swim back was a relief, and with the current behind, fast too.

The swim was over. I hadn't drowned, which felt like an achievement.

Iain

I wish something interesting had happened on the bike to make this section a better read, but it was very uneventful.

The bike route was pretty flat. The long climbs aren't very steep, and the steep climbs aren't very long. The first 30 miles are the best part of the course- suitable road surfaces and excellent views over the East Lothian countryside. The route back into Edinburgh had some 'interesting' sections – some cobbled roads, a farm road, and pavement.

The only issue I had was towards the end. There was a sharp left turn immediately followed by a slight rise in the road. A lot of people (including myself) misjudged which gear to be in. I heard a lot of "clanking" sounds as people tried to drop to a lower gear. Unfortunately, one of my clubmates broke his chain at this point.

Andrew

The bike route started in Prestonpans and then headed out through East Lothian, through Haddington and Gifford, before turning back and running in almost a straight line to Arthur's Seat in Edinburgh.

But it was only the direction that was straight. The elevation promised a course with very few flat sections and many ups and downs with some short sharp climbs.

And, because it was still windy, the course also added 25 miles into the wind as we came into Edinburgh.

The crowds were out in force, at least in the villages we passed. The largest town, Haddington, had the fewest spectators. Literally, one man and his dog. A man, and his dog, standing in his driveway. I can only guess the rest of the town must have been in church. Either that or the four-hour road closure on a Sunday morning wasn't appreciated by locals who decided to protest by staying away.

The course was varied, with plenty to see, from rolling hills to leafy hedges, to forest canopies, farmlands, and, at one point, one of my work's housing developments (which was nice to see, though not perhaps a selling point from anyone but me).

The final few miles saw a short burst of pave, the Edinburgh cobblestones, and then a climb around the back of Arthur's Seat. This comes as a shock after 54 miles but not as much of a shock as the sign at mile 40 that "This is the high point, it's all downhill from here!". Only it wasn't. Not in the slightest.

The last mile is downhill and provides a couple of minutes to relax, stop pedalling and getting focused on the run, or, in my case, to try and swallow an energy gel but forget how fast the road falls away and get tangled between attempting to eat the gel and desperately apply the brakes to slow down.

I read afterwards that some people complained the road wasn't in great condition and that there were a lot of punctures. I didn't see any more punctures than normal, and I thought the road was no better or worse than most Scottish roads.

I'd seen Iain in transition after the swim but couldn't see him in the run transition. I knew he was ahead of me, so I thought he must have left, so I decided to follow him out.

And, by quickly, I mean for around 500 metres. Then the climbing starts. One mile plus climb up Arthur's Seat.

This was going to be a long run…

The run route is deceptively hilly. Deceptive in that even the flats bit are steeper than you think. Especially on the third time around the four and a bit mile course.

The run-up Arthur's Seat was tough, but the course itself was varied and featured a long run through the Innocent Railway tunnel, lit by a spinning light show and soundtracked with classic rock.

It was worth racing Ironman Edinburgh just for the tunnel. Nothing beats running through a dark tunnel with AC/DC singing Highway To Hell and disco lights spinning around.

And then you have another hill. Followed by another hill. Then another hill. Then you finally get to run back down Arthur's Seat before you have to do it two more times.

It was tough.

Much tougher than expected, and I was pleased to get round in around 2 hours 10 minutes, so at least I was getting round in around 10 minutes a mile. Not great, but after the swim and bike, I was happy with it.

I finished the race with Iain. As it turned out, he'd been in the toilet, so I'd missed him in transition, but he caught me up, then paused, then slowed down at the end as I caught up with him. We finished the run together.

I wasn't sure if the announcer would shout: "You Are An Iron-man!" as we crossed the line. It seemed wrong; you should only get that for the full distance, but, as an IronMan event, I wondered if they'd also do it for 70.3.

They didn't. Instead, we had hardcore dance tracks. "Shake that ass! Shake that ass! Shake that ass!" it cried before the announcer quickly said, "Um, maybe that's the wrong song, let's get something more family-friendly".

Iain

I thought I was ahead of Andrew after the bike, so it was very disappointing to spot him ahead of me on the run. As he passed by, he shouted, "what lap are you on?" I should have said "my last!" As that would have played mind games with him.

I spent the next couple of miles trying to work out when he'd passed me on the bike, but I concluded that it must have been in transition as I'd gone to the loo.

I aimed to do run two laps and then walk the last one. Thankfully I caught up and passed Andrew on the second lap. If he'd kept ahead of me until the last lap, then I wouldn't have caught him.

At one point, a man ran next to me. He muttered "nearly" after every footstep. He kept this up for the mile he was alongside me. Eventually, he ran off. I wonder if he kept up his muttering until the end, and then did he mutter "done?"

Andrew was only a minute behind me on the third lap, so I slowed down and let him catch up. Better to walk down the finish line with him than do it on my own. Nothing whatsoever to do with getting to spend the last mile gloating about beating him at all three disciplines.

The event was well run, and I got home in time for my dinner. What more can you ask for in a race?

Andrew

Not all races can be reached from your front door. Sometimes you want to race somewhere spectacular, and, for me, that was San Francisco and the chance to swim from Alcatraz Island, the home of the infamous prison. Unfortunately, we'd no sooner got to San Francisco when:

"Have you got the key?" My wife asked.

"Yes," I said, closing the door to the flat.

I patted my pocket.

Nothing.

"Wait a minute…"

I tried the door. It was locked.

"When I said I had the key…"

This was not how the day was meant to begin.

This was our first full day in San Francisco, having arrived the day before after a 15-hour journey from Glasgow. So, after crashing out soon after we arrived, today was our chance to explore the city and, after waking at 2 am, then 3 am, then getting up at 4 am due to the jet lag, we were ready to pop out at 7 am and get breakfast when the nearest shop opened.

"Are you taking your phone?"

"No, I won't need it."

"Are you taking your wallet?"

"I've got the cash."

"Have you got the keys?"

"Of course!"

I didn't.

It's 7 am. We're trapped outside our flat, and the only thing to do is to sit on a children's swing outside and wonder if a ladder we found next to our flat will extend to the first-floor window we'd left open.

I can see myself reaching through the window, sliding in and opening the door.

I can see myself getting shot by a policeman for breaking and entering.

I ditch the ladder plan.

I have a better plan.

We will use the cash to get a train to the city centre to find an Apple store with free internet access and computers ready to use (they say sell, but everyone knows an Apple store is just a pretentious internet café), send an email to our landlords for the week and get spare keys from them.

It was full proof except we didn't know how to get a train, get to the city centre, or find an Apple store.

But that's what true grit is all about. Bear Grylls would be proud.

So, using all our guile, guts and ingenuity, we wandered the streets until we spotted a station, then wondered the city centre until we spotted some 'posh shops' then narrowed down our search to a few blocks on the basis that Apple always has a shop in the posh part of town.

Bear Grylls may follow rivers to find his escape; we followed the Gucci, Tiffanys and Luis Vuitton.

I should have a show in which I explain how luxury items can be used to help survive difficult locations – which, to be honest, is no different to Bear's shows and his secret luxury caravan, but at least I'd be honest about it.

So, five hours later, after a ride in a cable car and a Pain Au Chocolat in the world-famous Tartine Bakery, after such hard, harsh, desperate struggles, we finally got back into our flat, and I only hope that escaping from Alcatraz is easier than breaking into an Airbnb.

"Athletes, listen, this is an important announcement! You must – "

Pffffftt. Ziiipppp. Fffffuutttt. PA broken. Silence.

I'm waiting in transition. I'm wearing a wetsuit and trainers. I should be swimming in San Francisco bay, but I'm not – Escape From Alcatraz swim has been cancelled (for the first time), and I'm waiting to find out what happens next.

It was an early start, 4 am alarm, but with the time difference between the UK and the US, it still felt like mid-morning. I got an Uber to transition, having left my bike there yesterday, the first time they've let people rack up on a Saturday. I didn't know at this point it wasn't the only weekend 'first'.

At transition, I have plenty of time to set up my gear (unroll towel, check bike helmet, 10 seconds, done), check the bike for air (press both tyres down with my thumb, 5 seconds each) and then catch a bus to the boat which takes you out to Alcatraz (just a couple of minutes to catch the bus).

The last bus leaves at 6 am, but, as I wasn't sure of queues, I'd got to transition early and after completing my rigorous and thorough transition routine… I was on the bus by 5 am, which was too early. I was on the boat by 5:30 and had two hours to wait until the swim started.

On the boat, a former sternwheeler, you get divided by age: over 40 onto the top deck, under 40 on the main deck. In case you forget how old you are, you can check your leg: at registration, they write your age in black marker on your left hamstring.

I was under 40, and with my memory intact, I didn't even need to check when asked, so I got to sit on the main deck. As I'm there early, there's plenty of places to sit, so I sit down.

"Sorry, you can't sit there."

The man to my left is indicating a space of 10 metres.

"My friend's just coming back."

"It's okay. I'm sure we'll both fit."

I sit down and then worry that a man with a 10-metre wide butt will sit on me. Luckily, when the friend returns, he has a normal-sized butt, as do the two others who later join us. Not that I was checking out butts. But how much room does one butt need?! Even Sir Mix-A-Lot, the world expert on big butts and a man who cannot lie, would have said there was room for plenty of butts on that part of the boat.

I closed my eyes. I listened to random conversations and

thought about the swim.

I was nervous. Scared. But I had a secret weapon. Last night I'd left a water bottle in the fridge, and I planned to pour it on my face and down my back before jumping into the bay. I think the cold water will help me acclimatise before I plunge in.

But I never get to check that theory. At 6:30 am, just as we're due to sail to the start, a man with a loudspeaker tells us to be quiet and to listen to the PA. The PA then tells us that there's been a "small craft advisory warning "and the "swim is cancelled".

There's a loud groan — a protest. We're asked to leave the boat, and it's still not clear why.

People talk about refunds. About ditching the whole event. One man says he can't run or ride a bike; the only reason he was here was for the swim. Others talk in foreign languages. People were travelling around the world to be here. And the swim, the iconic swim from Alcatraz back to San Francisco, is cancelled.

Now I know how Al Capone must have felt – there was no escape from Alcatraz today.

Later, I found out that the wind and current were too strong even for the safety boats. The small craft warning was that the kayaks and paddleboards who marshal the swim would not cope with the conditions. And if it was too dangerous for the safety boats, it was too dangerous for swimmers.

I'm disappointed. I'd travelled a quarter of the world to be here, but I know safety comes first. And, after seeing the bay later, with whitecaps heading east, up the bat, rather than west as normal, and with winds hitting 35mph, it was the right call.

We queue to get back on the buses. It takes nearly two hours to get everyone back to transition. We still don't know what's happening, but announcements say that a duathlon race will occur, and details will follow.

I keep warm by staying in my dry wetsuit. I thought of pouring the frozen water on my head just so I could have the Alcatraz experience, but that would have been a stupid idea.

At transition, the PA gave out just as the announcement of the new race was made: "Athletes, listen, this is an important announcement – you must – pfft."

We gather at the entrance instead as a loudspeaker is found. The organisers will send us out in waves. Pros first, then by number, five at a time, every 10 seconds, to ensure people are spread out along the course just as they would be if they'd completed the swim.

I finally take off my wetsuit and get ready to... ESCAPE FROM TRANSITION!

But before that, have you read the Mind Chimp by Dr Steve Peters? It's a good book, well, a good chapter, about sports psychology. I say chapter because after the first chapter explains his theory, the rest of the book explains his theory and then explains it again and again.

I can only imagine that Dr Steve Peters inner chimp wasn't an editor.

If you've not read it, the basic theory goes something like this: everyone has a chimp, but not in a Michael Jackson type way. He had an actual chimp. We have an inner chimp. A voice in our head that reacts emotionally to events. The book shows how to understand how your mind works and ignore negative thoughts like doubt and fear.

It also tells you to ignore losing (which reminds me that I should get a copy for Iain) and that you should approach each event on the basis that you can only judge it on how well you trained and how well you raced, and that position is not important.

Wise words because, after the swim was cancelled, I was disappointed, half thought of not finishing it. Why bother if it's not the full event?

But that was my chimp talking. Instead, I ignored my chimp and thought: "This is the race. There is no swim. You can only start what's before you. You were on the boat. You were ready to dive in. You can't do any more than what you've done. So, pull yourself together and get on that bike and get out and run!"

And I did.

And it was brilliant.

Even though I felt like a sausage.

Iain had loaned me a tri suit. Normally, I'd wear tri shorts and change into a cycling top for the bike and a new t-shirt for the run. But, this time, I was going 'full triathlete'.

But what they don't tell you about 'full triathlete' is that 'full triathlete' involves a garment, the tri suit, which is designed to be slim, sleek, figure-hugging and aerodynamic. Or, if you're a normal body shape, designed to make you look like a strong man has just squeezed a sausage. A plump sausage.

I will not be posting any pictures from the race of anything other than my head!

The bike course is out and back from transition to Golden Gate Park. It's a closed road, which is fantastic, with great views of the bridge, Lands End, the west coast and Ocean Beach.

The hills are relatively shallow, but I was surprised at the number of people stopping and walking up to them. Maybe Scotland is better training for San Francisco than other places, but, if you are training somewhere flat, then practice for hills, the course goes up and down faster than a fat man on a trampoline.

For those travelling from the UK, India, Australia, the Caribbean, Malta and Cyprus (and anywhere else that drives on the left-hand side of the road), watch out for overtaking. Americans overtake on the left, not the right. This is more obvious when driving; the oncoming traffic is a big clue (!), but, on a closed road on a bike, it's easy to overtake on the right, and some folk don't like that. "Sorry!" to whoever I cut off at Cliff House, I don't know who you are, but you certainly had a loud voice!

The final few miles are flat, and, with a windy day and with the wind behind, it was a very quick finish before heading out on the run course. Not that I ran all of it.

Let's talk about hills. And steps. Hills are okay, you slow down, shorten your stride, switch your mind off and keep climbing. Steps, on the other hand, are made to be walked on. It's automatic. See a step. Walk on it.

At least that's my excuse for not running all the run routes. There are two sections with steps. The first at two miles, where you climb steps up to the Golden Gate bridge and the second at 4.5 miles, where you tackle the 'sand ladder'.

I'd read about the 'sand ladder' before the race. I knew it involved a steep climb after a short run on a beach, but I didn't realise just how steep it was. (Ladder should have been a clue, it wasn't called the sand stairs or the sand easy incline, it was the sand ladder). I didn't even try and run it. I grabbed one of the guide ropes at the side and used that to help me climb.

Once those two climbs are done, it's a nice two and a bit mile run back to transition on flat ground.

I played a game as I ran. As I said, at registration, everyone has their age written on their left hamstring with a black marker. I don't know why. Maybe the sharks in the bay want to know how old a leg is before they bite it off?

But, as I run, I check out people's legs to see how old they are. Then when they pass, I have a quick sideways look to see if they look older, younger or spot on.

It's a very judgemental version of Bruce Forsyth's Play Your Card Rights. Higher! Lower! Blimey, see a doctor. You've had a hard life!

It's only at the end that I realise that everyone could be doing the same for me. Except they'd add, I'd thought at his age he'd at least be trying to run the stairs?

At the finish, I got a big medal, a big meal (pasta, soup and various barbecue options) and a great sense of achievement – I could do no more than what I did, I was ready to jump, but better to be safe than to risk your life in dangerous waters. I'd escaped Alcatraz (albeit that maybe this year, the guards had left the keys in the lock to make it slightly easier).

Iain

"Dear Iain,

Welcome to Isklar Norseman – simply the ultimate triathlon on planet Earth

Now, sit down, breathe and go get a good cup of coffee or other. The more you relax, the easier securing your slot will be.

Because we have reserved a slot for you, we urge you to read our Race Manual once more to be sure that you understand the requirements and rules of the race."

I had finally won a place in Norseman but was it a win to have the opportunity to jump off a ferry into a freezing Norwegian fjord? Was it a win to have to bike 112 hilly miles? Was it a win to run up a mountain called zombie hill? Surely this should be the booby prize in a competition. The winner would get a week sunning themselves on a tropical island.

The more I thought about the race, the more I wanted to delete the email and pretend it hadn't happened.

What if I DNF'd?

What if I failed like when I first did the L'etape Du Tour? Like when Andrew did Norseman? Like when I did my first marathon? Like when I did my first, middle distance race?

Nobody needed to know I won a place. I could just say I failed to get in.

I did what any man does when faced with a problem. I ignored it! I decided to sleep on it and decide the next day.

The next day I woke up. I checked my email, and I entered the race.

I may fail, but at least I started.

Entering the race was the easy part. Once that was done, I had to arrange the logistics and decide how to train for it.

It was compulsory to have a support crew. I did this for Andrew when he did the race. That meant he owed me a favour. I phoned him and checked he'd do it for me. Thankfully he said yes.

The one logistic lesson we learnt from Andrew's attempt was that it was very difficult to do everything with just one support member. I decided to bring someone else – my girlfriend. The tricky part about this was we were due to get married six weeks before the race. Luckily, we had already agreed we would have a honeymoon but not until later in the year.

I told her that I thought we should have a break before then and wouldn't it be great to go to Norway. I told her all about the amazing scenery, people and waffles. She said it sounded great and agreed to come. I didn't mention the race or that Andrew was coming to. I'd leave that until after the wedding. She hopefully wouldn't divorce me.

There are two flights from Scotland to Norway. One goes from Edinburgh to Oslo, the other from Aberdeen to Bergen. Bergen is closer to Eidfjord, but Aberdeen was much further from my house. The time I saved driving in Norway would be lost driving in Scotland. I, therefore, booked a flight to Oslo.

Eidfjord is very small with limited accommodation, but I managed to arrange an Airbnb for a small village nearby – Ovre Eidfjord. I booked a chalet in Rjukan for the finish. The same one we had stayed at before. They sell great pizza on-site, which I was looking forward to having after the race.

With the logistics sorted, I had to now decide how to train for it.

My base swim fitness was poor. I had barely swum that year, but my swimming technique was good. I was confident that I wouldn't need to work much on technique once I got my stamina back.

My base bike fitness was good for short rides. I was commuting to work by bike four days a week (15 miles per day), and I would occasionally ride 30/40 miles at the weekend.

My base run fitness was okay for short races. I could run a 10k in 45 minutes, and I ran two or three times a week.

Up until 12 weeks from the race, I concentrated on improving my biking. I did this by increasing my commute and from work. I found longer ways to get to and from work. By the end, I was cycling 100 miles a week on just my commutes. I'd then do a long ride on a Sunday on top of that.

I tried to run three times a week. One 10k, one long run and one short easy run.

I joined a coached swim session once a week. It was a 2k swim, and I quickly got my stamina back.

Once I was 12 weeks out from the race, I added in longer rides/ runs.

I'd write one key thing I had to do each week in each discipline into my calendar and then try and fit it into my week where I could. I prefer time over distance as a measure for long runs and rides, so my week might say something like:

Week 1: 2hr run, 5-hour bike, 40 min swim

Week 2: 2.5hr run, 5-hour bike, 45 min swim

Each week would be different from the last. Sometimes a bit harder, sometimes a bit easier.

This way of training worked for me. It meant I could fit the training around my life rather than my life around training.

By the time the race came around, I'd ridden 2,720.5 mi. If I was to ride 2,720.5 miles from Glasgow, I'd end up in Baghdad in Iraq.

I'd ridden for 184 hours and 41 minutes. 184 hours is a long time to be biking. I could have used that time to learn to paint, speak a foreign language or, more likely, and I'd just watch television. 184 hours of TV means I could have binge-watched:

All of Game of Thrones (63 hours)

All of Breaking Bad (62 hours)

Every Marvel film (36 hours)

Every Harry Potter film (22 hours)

One episode of love island. (1 hour)

During my rides, I climbed 100,682 ft. This is the equivalent of cycling three times the height of Everest, which sounded impressive until I looked up the record number of climbs of Everest. Kami Rita Sherpa has summited 22 times. So, my paltry three times is just a walk in the park to him.

In terms of running, I covered 544.1 mi. Which is slightly more than the Proclaimers walked in in the song 500 Miles. However, they did walk 500 more afterwards.

In terms of swimming, I swam 40,808m. Whilst training for an Olympics, Michael Phelps would swim 80,000m a week. That's 1600 laps of a 50m swimming pool. I managed half a week of his training in six months. Which is why I don't have any Olympic medals, but how many episodes of Love Island as he watched? I bet it's none. I've seen one (see my bike stats).

Who's the success now?! Umm, probably still him.

I reached the start line fit, injury-free, and my wife didn't divorce me when I told her about Norseman. I can't ask for any more than that.

The flight to Oslo took two hours, but the wait in the airport for luggage took longer. My luggage could have flown back in the time it took to arrive. This also happened the last time I came to Norway.

The strange thing about the airport is the number of unattended bags lying around. Even stranger is what's in them. I saw cages containing cats and dogs left at the side of the luggage hall, seemingly without owners.

Once we collected the bags, we went to collect our car. This involved another long wait. The airport was proving to be more arduous than the race.

Thankfully we only had a short drive to our first hotel. A nice three-bed apartment in Geilo. This was a great place. It was very quiet and recently refurbished. We had dinner in a local restaurant. At this point, I'd like to apologise to Santa as I must admit I ate a local delicacy - reindeer. I hope it wasn't Rudolph,

It was one of the best dinners I ever had. The red nose was the tastiest bit....just joking. The only downside was the cost. Three main meals, two desserts, two beers and coke came to £140.

All the food in Norway tasted amazing. If the food didn't bring a tear (of joy) to your eye, then the bill almost certainly will. There's no such thing as a free meal here.

A famous quote says travel is the only thing you'll spend money on but come back richer for doing so. They must have never been to Norway. You may have great experiences, but you will definitively feel very, very poor.

The next day we drove to Eidfjord. I was told to phone a number to let the host know once we had arrived. I did. There was no answer. I tried again and again and again. There was still no answer. Eventually, we spotted a woman walking the street. I stopped her to ask for help. She said yes, she could help – she was the owner.

I asked her why she hadn't answered the phone. She replied that the number I was told to call was incorrect. She meant to change it but had forgotten. Who knows how we would have got in if we hadn't come across her?

The accommodation was a bit of a dump. I think it must have been converted from a shop as the layout was strange. It had big display windows and lighting that was so harsh it could only have been used to easily spot shoplifters.

It was fine for our purpose, i.e. it was close enough to Eidfjord to get to the ferry on time, but it isn't somewhere you'd book if you were after a romantic getaway.

The day before the race, I was surprisingly calm. I knew I'd done all the training that I could. I knew I was fit and healthy. I had a feeling that I was going to finish. All I had to do was trust in myself.

So instead of spending the day worrying, I went for a swim.

The organisers of the race put on a practice swim in the harbour. It was my first chance to see my fellow computers. My God. They all look like professional athletes. There wasn't an inch of body fat on any of them.

I'm slim, but I have a belly. I like beer and cake. This was the fittest I'd ever been, and I still didn't look anything like these Norse Gods.

I decided that I would intimidate them with the only thing I could do better than them – handling cold water. Coming from Scotland, I'm used to swimming in low temperatures. Whilst they all got changed into swimsuits, and gloves, and hats. I got changed into just my trunks.

It was quite warm – 13C, which is a reasonable temperature in Scotland. One man saw me swimming and started shouting. I couldn't make out what he said, but when I got out, he approached me and asked, "How could you do that?" I told him, "Don't worry, mate. I'm Scottish" He thought about it for a second and said, "like the salmon?"

That was the only time my swimming has ever been compared to a fish.

After the swim, I headed to registration. This process was quick and easy. I spent longer in the Norseman shop next to registration than in the registration. It's hard to go to a race and not buy the t-shirt, the cycling top, or the yellow duck dressed as a minion with a Norseman tattoo. This genuinely was for sale, and Andrew bought one.

After registration, a lot of the athletes started preparing for the race. Some were practising their bike transitions; some were going over roles with their support crew. We had an Ice cream and went to visit a waterfall. Later in the day, we went to a presentation from the race organisers about the race.

Andrew

"Dearly beloved, we are gathered here today to witness the union of swim, bike and run."

With these words, the race director opened the Norseman briefing the day before the race. However, he missed one important element. Triathlon is not just the union of swimming, cycling and running. It's also the union of athletes and supporters. The race is unsupported by the organisers, so every athlete needs their team on course to feed them, clothe them, pick up their swimsuit and bike after them and generally support them throughout.

Throughout Iain's race, I'll mention some of the things I learnt.

Iain

That evening we had a nice dinner and some beer. Some people are surprised that I have a beer before a race, but my view is that as I am not going to win the event. I might as well enjoy my holiday.

The race started at 5 am, which meant getting up at 2:30 am to board the ferry at 4 am.

Andrew

It was an early start. I hadn't slept well. Iain had booked accommodation with no curtains. I now know how hard it is to get to sleep in a country where the sun rises in April and sunset is October. Groan. I was so, so tired...

Iain

At 4:45 am, I jumped from the ferry and entered the water using what could only be described as a belly flop. I didn't see many other people use this technique. Possibly because upon my entry, most of the fjord ended up on the ferry.

It was a short swim to the start line. The water felt warm. There was a nervous energy in the air but a sense of anticipation.

Drones flew above me, filming the start for the inevitable video. I briefly wondered if I'd be on it. Maybe they will do a video for the wooden spoon racers.

A whistle or horn started the race. I can't remember which. I immediately got into my swimming rhythm. I kept a steady pace for the swim. It was very easy to sight the route. I kept the land 20m to the side of me and followed the coastline back to town. Occasionally the water would get very cold. I suspect that was the points streams were entering the fjord.

I didn't draft on anyone's feet. I hate swimming behind someone. I consider it is cheating. If you rode behind someone on the bike leg, you'd be disqualified, yet it's encouraged when swimming. I prefer to do the race myself. I will make it to the end without drafting anyone.

After an hour of swimming, I was close to Eidfjord. I could see a fire on the edge of town. I head to reach this and then turn left to get to the harbour. As I got close, I could start to make out people at the side of the swim. Some would shout, some took pictures. It was nice to see people. I wondered if Andrew and my Wife were watching or whether they'd taken the opportunity to go and get pancakes instead.

Finally, I reached the exit. I kicked my legs fast to try and fire them up to get ready to be back on land. I stood up and promptly fell face-first back into the water. I always struggle with staying upright after a swim. I paused for a minute and then tried again. I fell over. A man appeared and gave me a hand up.

I ran into transition, where my wife met me. She said she'd won a bet with Andrew as she thought I'd be out in 80 minutes. He thought it would be at least 90. I was out in 79 minutes.

Transition is a small area next to the harbour. There is no privacy here. If you want to know what a bunch of triathletes look like naked, then come to Norseman and stand near the harbour. My wife was so distracted that I mostly had to get changed by myself.

I changed into my kit, kissed my wife and then high fived Andrew. I started cycling. Only 112 miles of biking to go... oh feck. Have I forgotten my tracker?

The tracker is the thing that records my position on the course. It's the one thing I need to always have on me. Feck. Double feck. I'd forgotten it.

Andrew

Iain had not forgotten his tracker. We had put it on him. We wee a good support crew.

There was no need to rush out of Eidfjord once Iain left transition. It takes at least an hour to clear the first climb and reach the start of the route, where support is allowed. I had a nap and then some breakfast. This let the traffic clear, and I then followed up the mountain.

Iain

Oh well. I decided to carry on. I'll shout abuse at my support crew at the first stop and blame them. I did shout at them. They pointed at my foot where the tracker was. I felt a bit silly.

The bike leg starts with a 40K climb. I'd broken all the climbs down into units of measurement known as "crow roads" The Crow Road is a climb starting at the back of my house up the side of the Campsie Hills.

I find cycling more manageable if I break objectives down into things I know I can do. The first climb is five Crow Roads. Similarly, for the flatter section, I'd think of in terms of how many commutes to work it would be. My normal commute to work is an 8-mile cycle, so I'd calculate how many commutes to the next town when cycling the plateau.

This made the experience manageable, but I do not particularly enjoy long bike rides, so it was a struggle. My support team said I was like a stroppy teenager. One minute I'd be demanding a banana, but then as soon as they got one, I'd say, "Why'd you get me a banana. I wanted an apple!"

Because I don't ride long distances often enough, I also struggle to refuel on the bike. I prefer to stop at a cake shop and enjoy a break, so I did the same here and enjoyed a particularly good Bakewell tart from a shop in Geilo.

Other food delights on the bike (other than gels and bars) were a Twix, a chocolate brownie and lots of sports gels.

Andrew

During the bike leg, Iain got very hungry. He demanded every food type he could think of to escape the monotony of another energy gel. "Bring me a steak sandwich!", "I want a black forest gateau!", "Where's my swan?".

A good alternative to energy gels is a small bit of grated cheese. I bought some and intended to give them to Iain. The flavour of the cheese is good for resetting taste buds and provide a contrast to the rest of what he had eaten eat. Top tip though – don't store the grated cheese in a plastic bag in the car. I did. It soon becomes a big ball of melted cheese.

Iain

I had bought a new bike for Norseman. I hadn't intended to. A couple of weeks before the race, I'd seen a Facebook advert for a Cervelo TT bike which was set up perfectly for hilly courses. It was also unbelievably cheap.

I went round to see it. I asked the man selling it why it was so cheap. He said it was because his wife would only allow him to get another if he sold one of the eight (yes eight) bikes he already owned. I guessed from this money was not an issue for him!

I'd ridden it once before Norseman. I know "experts" claim don't do anything new on race day, but I've always taken the view "why not?" A bike is a bike. It's not vastly different to anything else I've ever ridden. What is the worst that can happen?

I spent the first half of the race with a very sore neck. Ahhh... that's the worst that could happen. It was annoying but thankfully cleared up as the race progressed.

Mentally I was feeling pretty good. I admit my attitude to my support team sucked, but once I get in the zone for a task, I get very logical and blunt. The emotional side of my brain just shuts down as I concentrate on what I need to do to complete a task.

The last section of the bike is mostly downhill. I zoomed along, confident that I wasn't last but also confident I was nowhere near the cut-off for going up the hill. As long as I kept going, I'd get a white t-shirt.

I pulled into transition. It was a small patch of grass by a lake. Andrew helped me get changed. He offered me an Ice Cream. I bet none of the other competitors stopped for a 99'er!

Andrew

I'd bought some ice cream in a local shop and had decided to taunt Iain with them. Expecting him to want one, but he refused as it was so unhealthy. He didn't let unhealthy stop him.

Iain

My aim for the run was to get to the bottom of Zombie Hill in 2hrs-ish and then walk from there. From that point, I could have a support runner.

I set off at a pace closer to walking than running. I was looking forward to having my wife join me on the run. It would be nice to speak to her, but she probably wasn't looking forward to speaking to me after my stroppiness!

The section to Zombie Hill is mostly flat. I felt good, and I managed to jog most of it, but I'd regularly stop whenever the support car appeared so I could get a quick drink. Andrew offered me more Ice Cream. I'm not sure where he was getting it all from.

Andrew

Whilst Iain ran very slowly towards zombie hill. We passed the time cheering the other athletes, but as we often stopped, we soon realised it was the same ones passing every time on the run route. The runners probably got tired of hearing my voice.

I didn't know any other athletes' names, so I named them myself. Big shout out in particular to "Nic Cage", who was the spitting image of Nic Cage. Big shout out to "The Walking Dead", who we were sure died on the bike but was still shuffling along the run route bent over and doubled up, and Stephen, whose actual name was Thomas and who was always just behind Iain, but we got his name wrong once and it then just stuck. Go, Stephen.

Iain

I made it to Zombie Hill in good time, and thankfully my wife was pleased to see me. She'd filled a bag with food, so we were good to go. I felt good, so we were able to walk quickly. I'd cycled zombie hill a few years previously, so I knew roughly what to expect when climbing.

The climb was an unrelenting slog, but the weather was nice, the air was cool, and I was feeling good. I never once thought about how far I had to go or how high. I just took it one step at a time. It's amazing what you can do by just living in the moment.

At the top of zombie hill, there was a checkpoint. The volunteers gave me some juice and checked I was not in the top 160. Thankfully I was not even close to 160. I got to head to the village finish rather than the summit finish.

It was 10K to the village and then ten laps of a loop outside the local hotel.

I made it to the village in good time and started the loops. I was going to finish. I took my time and walked each loop, savouring the atmosphere and the experience. I was here not because of 12 weeks of training but through years of hard work, trying new things, and not giving up when, at first, I did not succeed.

I finished because of Andrew and my wife.

We had all done this. It was not my achievement. It was our achievement.

Sharing the day with them was what made the day special. Not the jump, not the bike ride, not zombie hill.

Andrew and I stood together at the end. We had finished.

Iain Todd
Welcome to Isklar
Norseman Xtreme
Triathlon

EPILOGUE

Iain

Today is Sunday 17th October 2021.

We wrote the first draft of this book two years ago. I remember promising Andrew during Christmas 2019 that I'd complete another draft and then write an epilogue. Then I did... nothing.

Andrew

I wasn't surprised. I've seen his approach to training.

Iain

The book sat unfinished on my hard drive for nearly 18 months, which I realise is apt for a book called DNF. I couldn't finish it. Not that I didn't want to, but other things took priority. I don't need to point out that the world experienced a global pandemic. You probably noticed. It was in the news. However, we also had an upheaval on a personal level as our dad became unwell during that Christmas 2019 break. He was initially taken to his local hospital in the Western Isles before being transferred for further examination in Glasgow.

While there, he suffered from delirium – a horrible condition where he would see and imagine things that weren't there. For some, it can be a frightening experience. Still, he seemed to take it in his stride as he tried to filter the day's events in hospital through the visions he was seeing, often turning unexpectedly philosophical. One day when visiting him, he said, "it must be crap to be a door".

"What do you mean?" I asked.

"Who grows up wanting to be a door? Surely, you'd want a proper job!"

It was at this point I realised he was talking about his nurses. Due to his delirium, a nurse would sit in the doorway when we weren't around so that they could keep an eye on him. He thought the nurse's job was to be the door. And who would want to be a door?

While he was treated for delirium, he was sent to a nursing home back in the Western Isles to help him recover. And in Summer 2020. he returned home, and although he wasn't in the best of health, he lived happily until he passed away on 1st April 2021. A date that would have amused him.

Due to COVID restrictions, I only saw him once during this time. When we met, he was alert, and we had a good laugh talking about the time he asked, "Who grows up wanting to be a door?".

Andrew

I'm sad that I didn't hear him ask that question. If he had, and I'd been there, I would have been happy to have finally had the chance to ask him: "Do you want to hear the truth, or do you want a good story?"

I'm sure he would have asked for a good story.

Iain

Life went on. As lockdown eased, I returned to this book, our story, and thought of our dad's words again.

What is a door? Why would it be so bad to grow up wanting to be one? In a wall, a door is an exit. In a locked room, it is an escape. Why wouldn't you want to be a door?

We need doors in our life, just as we need hope, and I think to dream of becoming a door is to dream that life is about what we open, not what we close. I think that's the story he would have loved to hear and the message I want to share as I write these final words.

What is DNF? For me, it's not a door that has closed but one that is about to open.

Walk through your door and start your story.

Printed in Great Britain
by Amazon